ATTAINMENT'S
life skills curricula series

H O M E
COOKING

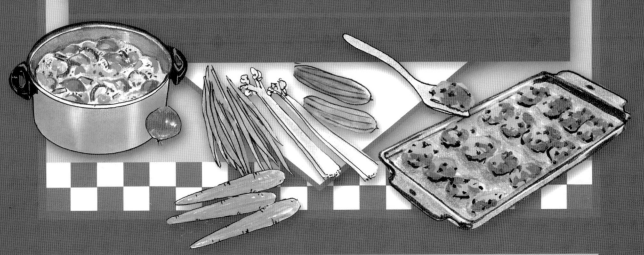

INSTRUCTOR'S GUIDE

Ellen Sudol, Author
Jo Reynolds, Illustrations
Dan Hanson, Editor
Sherry Pribbenow, Graphic Design

An Attainment Company Publication
©1992, 2006 Attainment Company, Inc. All rights reserved.
Printed in the United States of America
ISBN 1-57861-061-3

Attainment Company, Inc.
P.O. Box 930160 • Verona, Wisconsin 53593-0160 USA
Phone: 800-327-4269 • Fax: 800.942.3865
www.AttainmentCompany.com

Welcome to Home Cooking

Everybody likes to eat. It's even more fun when you've had a hand in preparing your own food. Mastering fundamental cooking skills is a big step toward independence and learning how to prepare fresh and wholesome food is an important consideration for good health. Learning some basic cooking skills is easy with Home Cooking. Just follow the step-by-step picture recipes and your students will be enjoying the results of some good Home Cooking before you know it.

The recipes featured in Home Cooking are practical and down-to-earth, yet flavorful and nutritious. The ingredients are common and easy to get, yet attractive and appetizing when served. Good cooking brings family and friends together in an atmosphere of camaraderie and good fellowship—and if you follow this curriculum, with a minimum of elbow grease.

The primary feature of Home Cooking is its unique, step-by-step picture cookbook. This curriculum shows you how to use it in class and how to encourage its independent use by students after they leave school. Reproducible Recipe Masters make it possible for you to have an endless supply of materials and for students to build their own cookbooks in your class.

Nonreaders and people with learning or memory problems can easily follow the pictorial sequences used in each recipe. The cookbook's picture index called the Menu Maker helps users find favorite dishes quickly—and independently—while the instructor's guide makes teaching cooking skills to any number of students a snap.

The unique Home Cooking Videos resurrect a slapstick style of humor and provide an entertaining yet informative element to instruction.

We hope you have big fun and good food and get as much as possible out of Home Cooking.

A Personal Note from the Author

Cooking for yourself is a major milestone on the road to an independent life. I know because I have seen it happen. Students who learn basic cooking skills are guaranteed a degree of independence that would previously have been unthinkable for them.

In 20 years of teaching home economics to adults with developmental disabilities, no single class has consistently proved to be as motivating as cooking skills. As a result of my experience, I created Look 'n Cook in 1986 and it continues to be a popular program. Partially because of its success and because I felt there was a need for a more advanced cooking program, I have created a new cookbook and curriculum: Home Cooking.

Like Look 'n Cook, Home Cooking evolved out of actual classroom experience, the trial and error discoveries from my years as a teacher. Unlike Look 'n Cook, it concentrates on fresh foods and teaching cooking from scratch. Recipes do not include the use of prepackaged goods.

I hope you find this program as useful as I have and that your students are equally motivated to learn new recipes and new skills. But most of all I hope you have fun sharing the results of these classic dishes.

Enjoy good cooking,

Ellen Sudol

Review of Materials

Recipe Set

- A 58 page full-color laminated cookbook — excellent for nonreaders and those with memory or learning problems. The 37 recipes featured here illustrate tasty traditional dishes. The laminated surface makes it easy to wipe off spills.
- Five rolls of durable plastic colored tape — allows you to color-code measuring cups and spoons and the stove and microwave you will be using. A simple color-coding system makes it easy for students to "read" cookbook recipes.
- An easel binder — allows you to prop the cookbook up for handy visual display when cooking.

Curriculum

- Instructor's guide — each lesson deals with basic cooking concepts. Students learn these key concepts by cooking actual cookbook recipes. Individual recipes combine to make complete meals. Learning to cook complete meals is a primary function of the curriculum and the focus of the lessons at the end of each chapter.
- Reproducible black and white Recipes — it's easy to photocopy recipes and distribute them to every student. Just add color to match the cookbook pages.
- Resource file — reproducible masters of the Meal Plans, the Home Cooking Report and fifteen Supplemental Recipes are stored separately here. The Meal Plans help students learn to prepare several recipes at the same time. The Home Cooking Report helps you keep track of each student's progress. The Supplemental Recipes let the creative instructor expand the program significantly.

Videos

- The Home Cooking videos are a sequel to Shopping Smart. They also stand on their own as a piece of instructional entertainment.
  Mary, played by Kari Elsner, bets her brother Carl that she can plan and cook a complete meal for five all by herself with her secret weapon, the Home Cooking Cookbook. Mary uses her wits and wiles — and her cookbook — to foil Carl's every sneaky attempt to fix the bet in his favor. The stakes are high: the loser has to do the dishes. Guess who wins? We're not telling, you'll have to watch it yourself.

Steps to Set Up Home Cooking for Classroom Training

Home Cooking is a big hit with novice cooks. By making basic cooking skills accessible to all students, it builds self-esteem and allows everyone to be successful. When working in class, refer to students as "cooks" or "chefs".

When they finish each lesson, students are encouraged to take their own copy of the recipe home to keep. They may even choose to collect individual recipes and compile their own cookbook.

The following steps are suggested for setting this program up for classroom instruction. However, we realize that no two classes will be the same and that instructors are highly innovative professionals used to adapting materials to fit their individual needs. Consider these general recommendations and augment in ways that suit your situation.

1. **Ready the classroom.** Make copies of the day's recipe for every user in class. Fold the photocopied recipe page beneath the top line of step-by-step sequencing, slip a marker in it and leave it on each student's desk or work area.

2. **Ready your work area.** Set up cupboards: pots together in one storage area, lids in another. Put utensils to be used out on the countertop for display and convenience. Make sure you have everything needed for the lesson, including the recipe ingredients.

3. **Think cleanup from the start.** Let students know this isn't the Holiday Inn. If you cook, you clean, too. Keep towels and sponges handy to mop up messes that occur, and as you finish with ingredients, put them back in proper storage places. When possible, encourage students to wash, dry and return dishes, pots, pans and utensils to storage places.

4. **Introduce users to kitchen materials** and cooking issues gradually, as the curriculum does, one at a time. Don't overwhelm students by trying to teach them everything at once. Lessons are structured for the gradual introduction of cooking concepts and techniques.

Timer   **Bell**

5. **Dress for the part** and encourage users to do the same. Roll up your sleeves, slip on an apron—yeah, you guys, too—put your hair up or back if it's long and wash your hands. Now you look and feel like cooks.

6. **Decide who is going to buy food**, how food costs will be covered and whether or not shopping is an instructional part of your Home Cooking program. (Note: If you also have Attainment's Shopping Smart program, consider merging them on occasion to pick up cooking supplies. It makes a great instructional combination.)

7. **Cookbook pages are laminated to protect against spills** and to allow students to mark off finished steps. An alternative to marking off steps on the laminated cookbook is to do it on the photocopied sheets instead.

8. **If students use photocopies to mark off completed steps, hand out two of each recipe** so they can take the clean copy home. You may want to encourage users to build their own personalized cookbooks by accumulating recipes learned in class. Consider including comments of praise on recipes sent home to indicate to caregivers that progress is being made.

9. **The quantities of food to buy and cook varies considerably.** How many students in class? What portions do the recipes call for? What can you afford? These are all pressing issues. While it depends on your resources and the scope of your program, most instructors will have some spending limits. If your class has 8-12 students, it probably won't be economical to prepare single portions for each cook. Often, there are diet restrictions as well that limit the amount some students can eat. However, nutritionists and frugal gourmets alike generally agree that a sampling of their results provides motivation for cooks. It isn't necessary or efficient to prepare large quantities, but a little will go a long way.

Each recipe indicates service quantities ("serves 4") in the top right-hand corner for students who wish to try them at home. But in the classroom, the quantity of food to be prepared is up to the discretion of the instructor, based on budget, number of students, and other factors.

It is recommended, though, that students get to taste their meals. Simply call it a"tasting" or a "snack" and give each student a small quantity of the finished product.

10. **If the class has 4 or more students, consider the Making Meals Lessons at the end of each chapter.** Here, several recipes are combined to make a complete meal. That way, each student or small group of students can learn one recipe at a time while the whole class works together to make a nutritious and tasty meal.

11. **Constantly emphasize safety measures** and incorporate them into every recipe where it is appropriate. They include use of sharp knives, electric appliances and oven mitts.

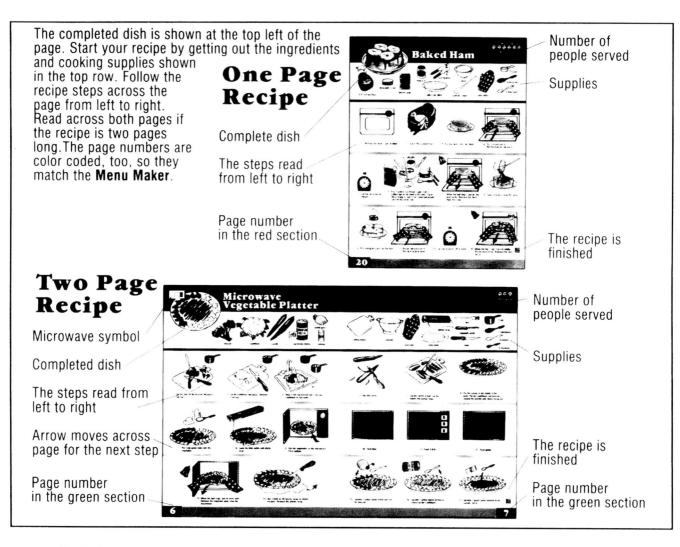

12. **Orient users to the layout of each cookbook recipe:** the ingredients and utensils are noted above the line, while the recipe steps are below the line. Encourage them to learn how to "read" the picture cookbook step-by-step.

13. **Each recipe step is presented in picture form (step pages) with minimal text.** They are designed to provide visually sequenced instructions. Follow and complete each step. Then cross the step out with the crayon and move on to the next step. In single page recipes the steps are left to right, top to bottom; double page recipe steps read from left to right across the fold of the facing pages. Steps are numbered.

14. **Discuss why some Home Cooking recipes have two pages.** Two page recipes always appear on facing pages with steps that proceed left to right across the fold.

Introduction to Home Cooking Curriculum

With Home Cooking there is no waste of instructional time. Every lesson has a recipe and every recipe has a purpose. Students learn basic cooking skills and concepts while learning basic, wholesome recipes. They learn by doing. So roll up your sleeves, because Home Cooking is about as hands-on as it gets.

Some lessons zero in on cooking concepts, like boiling, frying and roasting. Some focus on cooking techniques, such as how to safely cut or peel vegetables, and how to use a timer. Others concentrate on use of program materials: e.g., how to use the cookbook and color-coding cups and spoons.

Another key feature of Home Cooking is that recipes combine to form complete and balanced, nutritious meals. By learning how to cook several dishes at once, using a simple timing procedure, students can eventually master the skill of planning and cooking meals on their own. A series of "Meal Plans" are included in the Resource File to help users learn how to cook several dishes concurrently. Meal Plans provide sequenced picture instructions that users must follow when moving from one recipe to another.

It is necessary to have two timers available when performing the meal segments of Home Cooking. Either use two hand-held timers, or one hand-held and one built-in stove timer. If using two hand-held ones, place each on a photocopy of its recipe to remind users which one it applies to. (Note: Even if your training stove has a built-in timer, it is best to get two hand-held ones and use as suggested above. There are some Meal Plans that could make use of three timers, including the built-in one.)

Complete meal recipes can be performed one of two ways: "simultaneously", or "in order". While the goal for most users will be to learn simultaneous execution of meal recipes, for some it will remain an elusive and unreachable goal. Those students can choose the option of performing recipes in order.

"Simultaneous" is defined as concurrent preparation of more than one recipe with the use of two hand-held timers or one hand-held and one built-in stove timer. "In order" is also defined as making a meal involving more than one recipe; but here recipes are performed one at a time, starting with the one that takes the most to the one that takes the least amount of time. Meal Plans illustrate simultaneous recipe preparation.

Instructors should note that every oven range and microwave is different when it comes to cooking times. The longer the cooking time called for in a recipe, the greater the discrepancy will be between your unit and the cookbook. You can easily adjust the cookbook with the Marking Set. Use the Arrowhead marker until cooking times reflect the working of your stove. Or if your stove consistently operates at a higher or lower temperature than those called for in recipes, adjust color-coded tape accordingly.

Each lesson has a two sets of objectives that relate to specific skill areas. Primary Objectives target new concepts and techniques taught in each lesson, while Secondary Objectives refer to the recipe and include maintenance of skills learned in previous lessons. Once an instructional issue has been covered in a lesson, subsequent maintenance of that skill becomes a Secondary Objective. The time to instruct each skill or concept area—e.g., "using color-coded cups and spoons," is when it is highlighted in a lesson, e.g., "Lesson 2, Color-Coded Measurements". But some skills are needed in almost every lesson, like timer use and color-coding. Either the instructor performs the skill for users or assists them in performing it until it appears in a lesson.

When recipes combine to make meals, only Primary Objectives are provided, and address the challenge of performing several recipes either simultaneously or in order.

Two narrative sections appear in each lesson and pinpoint the "message" or instructional value of the recipe. Lesson narratives, like Primary Objectives, relate to cooking concepts and techniques, while Recipe Narratives relate to the recipe.

A Training Suggestions segment offers some helpful hints to consider using during initial stages of instruction. Unlike Objectives and Narratives, Training Suggestions include both recipes and cooking techniques. Innovative instructors will undoubtedly add their own inventive training methods as they become familiar with the program. Tailor the program to meet your needs: number and types of students, length of class, funding resources and kitchen equipment—these are all major considerations.

Some Training Suggestions relate to the recipe at hand, while others are more general and involve use of the Home Cooking program. The recipe-specific suggestions appear at the end of each lesson.

Resource File Contents

The Resource File includes masters (for you to photocopy) of **Meal Plans**, the **Home Cooking Report**, and **Supplemental Recipes**.

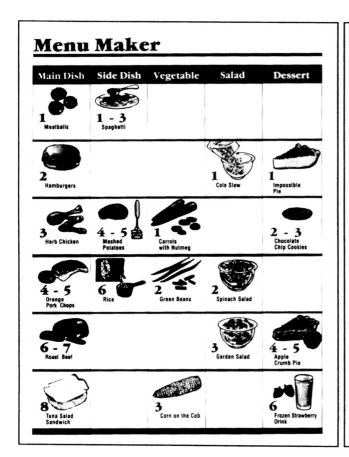

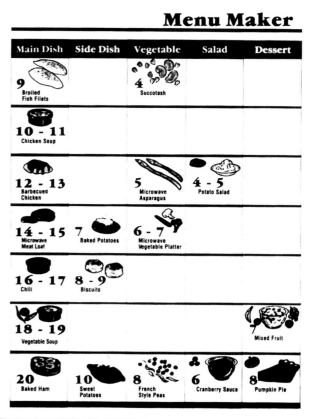

6

The **Meal Plans** illustrate how to prepare several recipes at the same time. Planning and making a complete meal is the focus of the lessons found at the end of each chapter. The recipes chosen for the Meal Plans reflect those in the **Menu Maker**—which is in the introduction to the Cookbook and is illustrated on page 6. The Menu Maker works like a matrix. Meals read across and single recipes read down. Desserts are not included in the Meal Plan.

The **Home Cooking Report** lets you record the "who, how, when and what" of a cooking class. The data sheet is especially helpful when setting and measuring progress toward specific cooking goals.

COOKING REPORT

page 1

Instructor _____

Class Period _____

Name	Date	Goal

Cooking Data Sheet Directions
The Data Sheet on the reverse side includes space to assess all aspects of a student's cooking performance. You may use all columns or select only the ones which are applicable.

Date and Name	Use one sheet per student or one sheet for each class.
Recipe	Title of recipe and page number in cookbook.
Lesson #	Number of lesson in the Instructor's Guide.
Recipe Steps	Each box represents a Home Cooking recipe step. Circle the box that corresponds to the last step of the chosen recipe to indicate the total number of steps in that recipe.
	Use Performance Scale code or simply check each box if a step is completed correctly.

PERFORMANCE SCALE	
I	Independent performance
V	Verbal prompts needed
P	Physical prompts needed
U	Unable to complete
	Did not participate

The **Supplemental Recipes** are listed below.
Photocopy; then color in the steps that require measurement or temperature selections.

Scrambled Eggs	Fried Eggs	Microwave Bacon
Oven French Toast	Pancakes	Egg Salad
Quick Pizza Rolls	Roast Cornish Hens	Sirloin Steak
Zucchini, Tomato & Onion	Broccoli	Mixed Vegetables
Butternut Squash	Cucumber Salad	Microwave Fish Filets (two pages)

Table of Contents

Microwave Cooking

Meal Planning

Using The Cookbook

Using The Cookbook

Recipe:

Spaghetti

Flash cards help students learn cookbook picture symbols.

Primary Objectives

1. Uses a color-coded stove, oven and electric frying pan.
2. Uses a timer.

Secondary Objectives

1. Knows that oven mitts are used for safety when removing anything from stove or microwave.
2. Follows a one page recipe that can be used with many different sauces and meats.

Teaching Suggestions

- Make flash cards of cookbook picture symbols, like the stove flame, using 3 x 5 index cards. Make one of the flame under a pot. Make others of program materials and utensils students will use: i.e., measuring cups and spoons, an electric frying pan, a timer, seasonings, etc. Ask students what the cards represent. Hand cards to everyone in class and ask them to match cards to actual items on counter. Or give all the cards to one student and ask him to match each to items on counter.

- Have users practice turning the stove on to red and off to white. Discuss the importance of this procedure and test the ability of each to perform this step.

- Discuss that a one pound box of spaghetti usually feeds about six people. If more servings are required extra noodles can be used with a larger pot and more water so that the timing remains the same.

- Pasta is the basis for many dishes, including macaroni & cheese, spaghetti, lasagna, casseroles and more. Discuss.

- Make sure students use oven mitts when carrying the pot to the sink to drain water off in colander. Discuss need for mitts.

- Introduce the timer and show users step #6. Have students practice setting it. Most timers have to be turned past ten and then set to the appropriate time.

Introduces the color-coded stove, and involves many other basic cookbook concepts that are detailed later, such as boiling, timer use, oven mitts and colander use. Point out the flame symbol that first appears on step #3. Inform students that the oven and electric frying pan are color-coded and will be used in future lessons.

Recipe Narrative

Spaghetti is a good recipe to start with because it's simple and straightforward.

Color-Coded Measurements

Recipe:

Spaghetti Sauce

1 cup - red

Ask students to identify correct measuring cup by color.

Primary Objectives

1. Chooses correct color-coded cup or spoon.
2. Measures recipe ingredients accurately.
3. Follows a two page recipe. Knows how to read facing pages following steps across the fold from left to right.

Secondary Objectives

1. Operates the color-coded stove.
2. Uses a food chopper on vegetables.
3. Operates a manual can opener.
4. Sets the timer to the number of minutes stated in the recipe.

Training Suggestions

● Do a flash card drill using the four spoons and one cup used in this recipe and asking students to pick the correct one for each step. Flash cards can be expanded to include all the measuring cups and spoons used in Home Cooking. These are standard in all recipes: encourage students to memorize them.

● Practice measuring sugar before beginning the recipe. Ask students to measure out all the amounts used in this recipe.

● Discuss how different kinds of canned tomatoes can be used for different effect. Use whole for a chunky sauce, or puree for a smooth sauce.

● If using fresh tomatoes, follow this procedure: put in boiling water for 30 seconds and let cool before removing skins and chopping into small pieces.

● Use a knife, fork and cutting board to chop vegetables, or use a food chopper, which is easier, safer and fun. (Note: Lesson 3 also deals with proper chopping procedure.)

● Adjust cooking time for up to 2 hours if desired. The longer it cooks the more it thickens.

*Introduces color-coded measuring cups and spoons to students.
Explain the role of color-coded measuring devices throughout
Home Cooking. Stress that measuring cups or spoons must be "full
but flat" in order to measure accurately.*

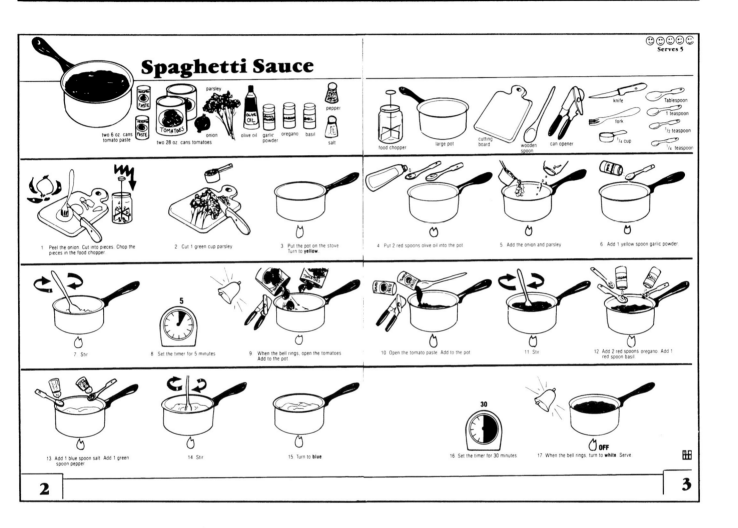

Spaghetti Sauce

Serves 5

two 6 oz cans tomato paste — two 28 oz cans tomatoes — parsley — onion — olive oil — garlic powder — oregano — basil — pepper — salt

food chopper — large pot — cutting board — wooden spoon — can opener — knife — fork — 1/4 cup — Tablespoon — 1 teaspoon — 1/2 teaspoon — 1/4 teaspoon

1. Peel the onion. Cut into pieces. Chop the pieces in the food chopper.
2. Cut 1 green cup parsley
3. Put the pot on the stove. Turn to **yellow**.
4. Put 2 red spoons olive oil into the pot
5. Add the onion and parsley
6. Add 1 yellow spoon garlic powder.
7. Stir
8. Set the timer for 5 minutes
9. When the bell rings, open the tomatoes. Add to the pot.
10. Open the tomato paste. Add to the pot.
11. Stir
12. Add 2 red spoons oregano. Add 1 red spoon basil.
13. Add 1 blue spoon salt. Add 1 green spoon pepper.
14. Stir
15. Turn to **blue**
16. Set the timer for 30 minutes
17. When the bell rings, turn to **white**. Serve.

2

3

Recipe Narrative

This is a basic tomato sauce recipe that can be used over pasta with or without meatballs. It's always a good idea to make a large amount of sauce, since it freezes well and can be defrosted and reheated in a microwave. And this recipe is low in calories and fat.

11

Kitchen Safety

Recipe:

Meatballs

Demonstrate correct use of utensils when chopping items.

Primary Objectives

1. Operates an electric frying pan.
2. Removes electric component of frying pan before immersing it in water.
3. Knows that water and electricity are a life-threatening combination and that hands must be dry when plugging into or out of an outlet.
4. Uses a fork, knife and cutting board when cutting or chopping food.
5. Operates a manual food chopper or food processor safely.
6. Uses oven mitts when putting food in or taking it out of oven or microwave, or handling anything hot.

Secondary Objectives

1. Measures ingredients accurately.
2. Stirs ingredients together.
3. Operates the color-coded electric frying pan or color-coded stove.
4. Sets timer correctly.
5. Rolls a measured amount of meat into a ball.

Teaching Suggestions

- Color-code an electric frying pan: red—high; yellow—medium; blue—low; off—white. Discuss the importance of kitchen safety.

- Demonstrate proper use of the color-coded electric frying pan: plug the electrical component into the pan and plug the cord into wall socket before turning on and turn the pan off before unplugging.

- Discuss issues involved with use of electrical equipment.
  If you don't have an electric frying pan, use a different appliance, like a blender.
  Issue: Students should always have dry hands when plugging an outlet into a wall socket. Issue: an appliance shouldn't be immersed in water until the electrical component is removed. Issue: when washing, allow the pan to cool before removing the electrical component to wash.

Introduces kitchen safety precautions that are practiced throughout this program. Kitchen work can involve any number of hazards and requires students to learn safety measures. These include cutting, chopping or peeling food, removing hot dishes from a stove or microwave and using and washing electric appliances.

- Demonstrate correct use of knife, fork and cutting board when chopping food items. Show how to use a fork to hold onion when cutting it with a knife. Point out that manual food choppers and food processors are alternatives.

- Introduce oven mitt use and discuss their role in preventing burns when removing pots and pans from oven or microwave. Point out that they should always be used when handling anything hot. Rule: if in doubt wear them.

- Although the recipe calls for lean ground beef, ground turkey can be used as a substitute.

- Meatballs can be made without oregano and garlic powder if a less spicy version is desired.

Recipe Narrative

Combine meatballs with spaghetti sauce or another kind of sauce. Meatballs can be prepared ahead of time and frozen. Simply add the frozen meatballs to the spaghetti sauce and cook until heated through.

13

Making Meals

Recipes:

Spaghetti

Spaghetti Sauce

Meatballs

Primary Objectives

1. Prepares a series of recipes simultaneously, or in order, starting with the one that takes the most to the one that takes the least amount of time.
2. Knows that preparing and freezing some recipes in advance is a great time saver. For example, spaghetti sauce and meatballs both freeze well and can be used in the same meal.
3. Follows the Meal Plan sequence for making meatballs and spaghetti.
4. Operates two timers--a hand-held one and the stove's built-in timer, or to use two hand-held ones.

Meal Plan—Simultaneously (using two timers)

1. Prepare meatballs from step #1 to end.
2. Begin spaghetti sauce—complete through step #16.
3. Do spaghetti recipe from beginning to end.
4. Turn the stove off when bell rings (spaghetti sauce recipe).
5. Add meatballs to spaghetti sauce.
6. Serve meal.

Variation—if frozen meatballs are used

1. Prepare spaghetti sauce through step #15 and add frozen meatballs.
2. Do step #16, spaghetti sauce.
3. Do spaghetti noodles.
4. Turn spaghetti sauce off (step #17) when timer rings.
5. Serve meal.

Meal Plan—In order

1. Meatballs
2. Spaghetti Sauce
3. Spaghetti

Teaching Suggestions

- When using two hand-held timers: place timers on top of a photocopy of corresponding recipes.
- Review basic cooking concepts taught in first three lessons: using a color-coded oven and measuring cups and spoons, use of oven mitts and timers, "reading" the cookbook, and using an electric frying pan safely.
- Review recipes taught in first three lessons, making spaghetti sauce, noodles and meatballs and discuss value of cooking a complete meal independently.
- Discuss freezing quantities of sauce and meatballs ahead of time and explain the "in order" cooking sequence. variation. This recipe loses little when prepared in order, since the food doesn't sit long enough to cool. Discuss the occasional need to reheat a dish.

Recipe Narrative

Spaghetti and meatballs is the first complete meal in the cookbook because it is a great basic dish that most people enjoy. It covers the spectrum of food groups, is easy to make and can be largely prepared in advance by freezing sauce and meatballs.

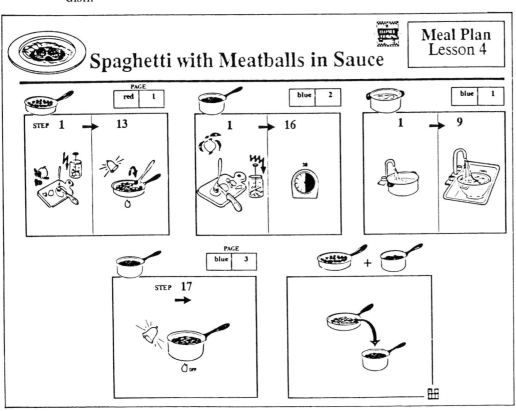

Spaghetti with Meatballs in Sauce — Meal Plan Lesson 4

Cooking Techniques

Lesson 5

Stirring

Recipe:

Chocolate Chip Cookies

Point out touching the bottom of the bowl with the spoon.

Primary Objectives

1. Operates the electric mixer safely.
2. Stirs ingredients together using a wooden spoon.

Secondary Objectives

1. Operates color-coded oven.
2. Measures ingredients accurately.
3. Sets timer correctly.
4. Uses oven mitts when putting cookie sheets in or taking out of oven.
5. Uses spatula to transfer the baked cookies from sheets to cooling racks.

Teaching Suggestions

- Demonstrate the following sequence of use: insert and remove beaters, then turn mixer on or off. Stress that mixer should never be plugged in when replacing beaters.
- Show a stirring motion using a bowl and wooden spoon. Point out the importance of touching the bottom of the bowl with the spoon when mixing ingredients together.
- Review turning oven on and off and the need to use mitts when putting something in or taking it out of the oven.
- Cookies are a "sometimes food" reserved for parties, holidays and special occasions. They also make a nice gift.

16

Introduces concept of stirring and use of an electric mixer and a wooden spoon. Raises and discusses some safety and precautionary measures.

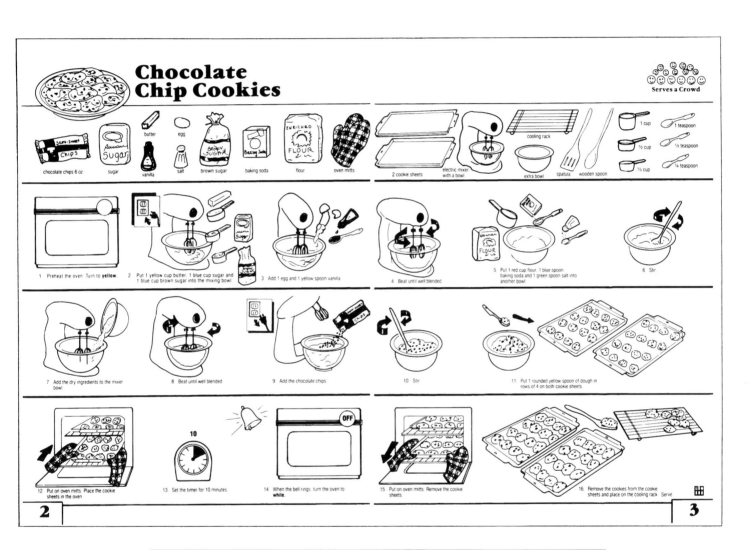

Recipe Narrative

The recipe can easily be increased by using the 6 oz. bag of chocolate chips and doubling all other ingredients. This would also reduce calories slightly. Add one-half cup each of raisins and chopped nuts if desired. Store cookies in an airtight container or in a freezer bag.

Lesson 6

Nonstick Equipment

Recipe:

Hamburgers

Nonstick equipment helps to reduce fat in our diets.

Primary Objectives

1. Learns to cook with nonstick equipment, such as frying pans and baking dishes.
2. Knows nonstick frying pans allow you to cook with little or no additional fat, making recipes lower in fat and calories.
2. Uses wooden or plastic tools when working with nonstick frying pans because metal scratches the surface.
3. Uses a nonabrasive scrub brush to clean nonstick cooking and baking pans.
4. Knows same principles apply to nonstick baking sheets.

Secondary Objectives

1. Measures ingredients accurately.
2. Uses knife, fork, cutting board and manual food chopper safely.
3. Cracks an egg.
4. Mixes ingredients.
5. Shapes hamburgers.
6. Operates color-coded stove.
7. Sets timer accurately.
8. Turns hamburgers over using spatula.

Teaching Suggestions

- Discuss reasons why it is good to reduce fats and cholesterol in our diets. Using nonstick equipment and lean ground beef reduces the fat content of the hamburgers.
- Explain that grills and broilers are acceptable alternatives when preparing hamburgers. Either allows fat from meat to drain off. The timing is the same.

Introduces nonstick kitchen equipment and features use of an electric frying pan in a hamburger recipe.

- Have students practice using a spatula. Demonstrate how to turn something over in the frying pan.
- Show students what excess fat looks like when it congeals. Ask them to think about having something like that in their stomachs and to comment on it. Have fun with it.

Recipe Narrative

This recipe insists on use of low fat meats cooked with little or no grease in the pan, reducing cholesterol and caloric intake. Use ground turkey in place of lean or extra lean ground beef and reduce the fat content even further.
(Note: Look carefully on the ground turkey package to see the percentage of fat content)

Lesson 7

Slicing

Recipe:

Carrots

or Apple Crumb Pie

Primary Objectives

1. Uses a knife and fork with a cutting board when slicing carrots or apples.
2. Peels carrots with a vegetable peeler.

Secondary Objectives

1. Operates the stove correctly.
2. Drains food in a colander using oven mitts for safety.
3. Sets timer accurately.
4. Measures ingredients accurately.
5. Knows to stir with a wooden spoon because the handle doesn't get hot.
6. Recognizes boiling liquids.

Teaching Suggestions

- Show students how to use a cutting board to protect counter and table tops.
- Demonstrate holding vegetables with a fork when slicing with a knife.
- Show the more dexterous students how to hold carrots between fingertips instead of using a fork. If dexterity is in question, insist that students use a fork when slicing vegetables.
- Demonstrate placing a colander in the sink when draining food and explain how use of oven mitts prevents steam burns.
- Quantities can be easily increased or decreased when preparing this recipe. Use dill as an alternative to nutmeg in the carrots.

Introduces vegetable peeler and uses it in preparing carrot recipe. Involves using a knife and fork to slice carrots after peeling. In this recipe, carrots are flavored with nutmeg instead of salt and butter so they are low in salt and fat yet tasty.

Apple Crumb Pie

Serves 8

6 apples · sugar · butter · lemon juice · flour · ENRICHED FLOUR · BROWN SUGAR · brown sugar · cinnamon · 9" frozen pie shell · oven mitts

cookie sheet · cutting board · bowl · small bowl · knife · peeler · fork · wooden spoon · 1/2 cup · 1/3 cup · 1/4 cup · Tablespoon · 1 teaspoon

1. Put the baking sheet into the oven. Turn to **red**.
2. Peel the apples.
3. Core and slice the apples.
4. Put 2 blue cups sugar in the bowl. Add 2 red spoons flour.
5. Add 1 yellow spoon cinnamon and 1 red spoon lemon juice.
6. Stir.
7. Add the apple slices.
8. Mix.
9. Spoon the apples into the pie shell.
10. Put 1 yellow cup flour in a small bowl. Add 1 green cup butter.
11. Add 1 green cup brown sugar.
12. Mix until crumbly.
13. Sprinkle the crumbs on the apples.
14. Put on oven mitts. Put the pie onto the baking sheet in the oven.
15. Set the timer for 40 minutes.
16. When the bell rings, turn to **white**. Put on oven mitts. Remove the pie on the baking sheet.
17. Set the timer for 55 minutes.
18. When the bell rings, slice and serve.

4   5

Recipe Narrative

Slicing and peeling apples are necessary steps in preparing apple crumb pie, so it's a good alternative recipe for this lesson. In the fall, it can also be used to demonstrate seasonal foods — Lesson Thirty-Five.

Lesson 8
Chopping & Grating Vegetables

Recipe:
Cole Slaw

It's safer to use a fork when grating vegetables.

Primary Objectives

1. Uses a knife, fork and cutting board to cut vegetables in half before chopping into smaller pieces.
2. Uses a food chopper to cut vegetables.
3. Knows that grating vegetables is an alternative to using food chopper or knife and fork.

Secondary Objectives

1. Peels onion.
2. Measures ingredients accurately.
3. Stirs ingredients.

Teaching Suggestions

- Ask users to name the various ways onions can be cut into smaller pieces. Then explain the different options, while demonstrating: first, cut the ends off and peel it by hand; then, using a cutting board, show how to chop off a piece of the onion. Second, show students how to use the food chopper. Then, demonstrate cutting an onion with a grater. Let users practice each method. Ask which option they prefer, and why.
- The following ingredients can be added to taste:
    2 tbs. raisins
    1\2 grated green pepper
    1 stalk grated celery
- Reduced calorie mayonnaise is recommended but regular can be used instead.

22

Presents more ways of rendering vegetables into smaller and smaller pieces. There are different methods for accomplishing the same goals, and which one a student uses depends on dexterity, ability to use electric food chopper safely and the availability of kitchen equipment .

Recipe Narrative

The recipe suggests using preshredded cabbage, because it's hard to shred with a knife or grater. Use a food processor if one is available.

Lesson 9

Peeling & Mashing

Recipe:

Mashed Potatoes

Demonstrate the use of a vegetable peeler.

Primary Objectives

1. Uses a vegetable peeler.
2. Uses a potato masher.

Secondary Objectives

1. Cuts potatoes into pieces.
2. Operates color-coded stove.
3. Measures ingredients accurately.
4. Sets timer correctly.
5. Recognizes boiling.

Teaching Suggestions

- Hold up vegetable peeler and potato masher for students to see and ask which recipes would require their use.
- Demonstrate use of vegetable peeler and potato masher in preparing this recipe and encourage students to try.
- Discuss advantages of using margarine in place of butter and skim as a substitute for whole milk.

24

Introduces use of potato masher. Vegetable peeler is also used.

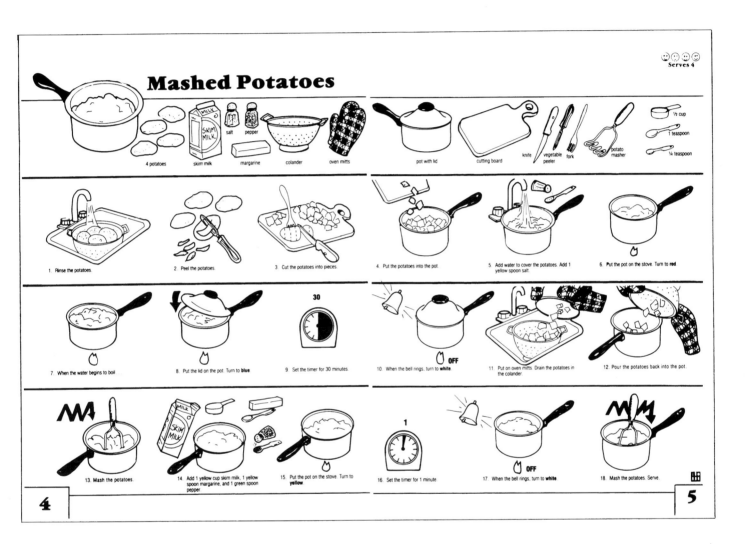

Recipe Narrative

The recipe calls for students to peel and cook potatoes before mashing. Students learn a sequence of vegetable preparation skills: peel, boil, drain in colander, add milk, butter and seasonings, reheat and mash to produce an appealingly fluffy result.

Using a Blender

Recipe:

Impossible Pie

or Frozen Strawberry Drink

Primary Objectives

1. Operates a blender safely.
2. Knows that blenders are used for pureeing, mixing, finely chopping small quantities and blending foods, especially liquids.
3. Disassembles and cleans the container portion of the blender.
4. Understands that the motor portion of blender can't be placed in water.
5. Understands the lid must be put on the blender before it's turned on.

Frozen Strawberry Drink

Serves 1

vanilla — skim milk — whole frozen unsweetened strawberries — sugar — glass — blender — 1/2 cup — 1/4 teaspoon — 1 teaspoon

1 Put 1 yellow cup skim milk in the blender

2 Add 1 yellow cup frozen strawberries

3 Add 1 green spoon vanilla

4 Add 1 yellow spoon sugar

5 Put the lid on the blender

6 Blend

7 When blended, pour into a glass. Serve.

6

Secondary Objectives

1. Operates the color-coded oven.
2. Measures ingredients accurately.
3. Sets the timer.
4. Uses oven mitts.

Teaching Suggestions

- Demonstrate plugging blender in and turning on and off. Caution students to keep the top on when operating blades and make sure they have ceased revolving before removing lid.

- After using, fill the container with water to soak it. When ready to clean, disassemble and warn students about the sharpness of blades (even when inactive). Also, indicate that the motor may not be placed in water when washing dishes. The housing should be cleaned with a damp sponge after unplugging.

- Additional sugar or a sugar substitute can be used in the frozen strawberry Drink.

- If fresh strawberries are used, then add three or four ice cubes for a thick shake, one or two for a thinner one.

Note: Frozen Strawberry Drink is the primary recipe for Lesson 21—Frozen Foods.

*P*resent the blender and discuss its use in pureeing, mixing, finely chopping and blending, such as in the recipe for impossible pie or frozen strawberry drink.

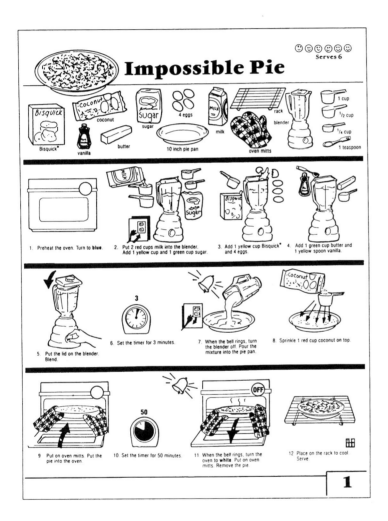

Impossible Pie
Serves 6

1. Preheat the oven. Turn to **blue**.
2. Put 2 red cups milk into the blender. Add 1 yellow cup and 1 green cup sugar.
3. Add 1 yellow cup Bisquick* and 4 eggs.
4. Add 1 green cup butter and 1 yellow spoon vanilla.
5. Put the lid on the blender. Blend.
6. Set the timer for 3 minutes.
7. When the bell rings, turn the blender off. Pour the mixture into the pie pan.
8. Sprinkle 1 red cup coconut on top.
9. Put on oven mitts. Put the pie into the oven.
10. Set the timer for 50 minutes.
11. When the bell rings, turn the oven to **white**. Put on oven mitts. Remove the pie.
12. Place on the rack to cool. Serve.

1

Recipe Narrative

Impossible pie is made with coconut and custard and forms its own crust while baking. It is very easy to prepare. If a low calorie dessert is preferred, substitute the strawberry drink as a tasty alternative.

Lesson 11

Making Meals

Recipes:

Herb Chicken

Mashed Potatoes

Carrots

Primary Objectives

1. Prepares a series of recipes simultaneously or in order from the one that takes the most to the one that takes the least amount of time.
2. Follows the Meal Plan below.
3. Operates two timers, a hand-held one and the built-in stove timer, or two hand-held ones.

Meal Plan—Simultaneously

1. Prepare the baked herb chicken through step #7 (remove the recipe page from the cookbook and place the set timer on the page. When the bell rings go back to the herb chicken recipe and complete it.)
2. Prepare mashed potatoes through step #5.
3. Prepare carrots with nutmeg through step #3.
4. Prepare mashed potatoes steps #6-9. Place the timer on the mashed potato recipe.
5. Prepare carrots steps #4-8. Use the same timer as the mashed potatoes—it should read approximately 20 minutes at this point.
6. When the bell rings shut off the stove for both potatoes and carrots. Carrots step #9 and mashed potatoes step #10.
7. Complete the carrot recipe steps #10-13.
8. Complete the potato recipe steps #11-18.
9. When the bell rings for the herb chicken, turn the oven off.
10. Serve the meal.

Meal Plan—In Order

1. Prepare the chicken.
2. Prepare the carrots.
3. Prepare the mashed potatoes.

Teaching Suggestions

- Divide the class into three groups, each preparing one dish.

- Direct student attentions to the other recipes being performed and orient them to the principle of simultaneous activity. This is a good way to introduce the concept of simultaneity.

- Encourage users to sample their success at the end of class. Call it a tasting, or sampling. It doesn't have to be much: just enough to appreciate their work.

- Watch the Home Cooking Video and discuss how Mary and Bruno shared responsibilty when they cooked this meal.

Making Meals

Recipes:

Hamburgers

Cole Slaw

Primary Objectives

1. Prepares two of recipes simultaneously or in order from the one that takes the most to the one that takes the least amount of time.
2. Follows the Meal Plan.

Meal Plan—In Order

This is one of the easiest meals to make in Home Cooking since no simultaneous recipe preparation is required.

1. Prepare the cole slaw in advance or immediately before starting the hamburgers.
2. Prepare the hamburgers.
3. Serve the meal.

Hamburgers with Cole Slaw

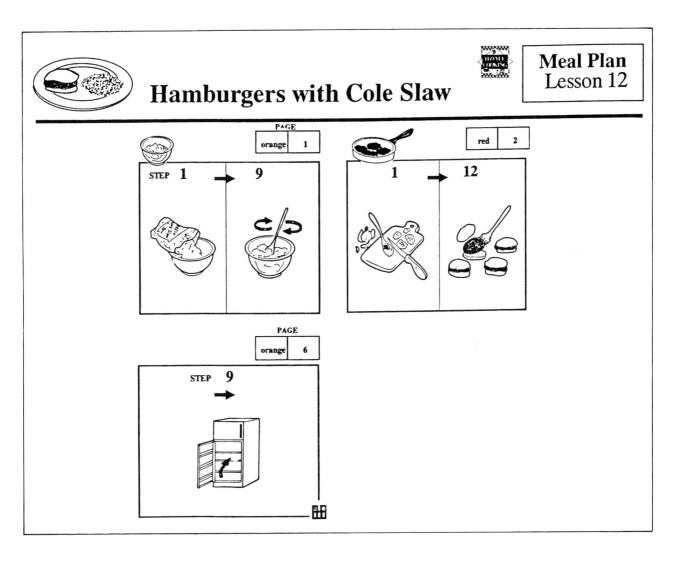

Cooking Methods

Lesson 13

Boiling

Recipe:

Rice

or Green Beans

Primary Objectives

1. Recognizes boiling liquids.
2. Understands that boiling means cooking food in liquid over high heat until bubbles begin rising to the surface.

Secondary Objectives

1. Measures ingredients accurately.
2. Operates color-coded stove.
3. Cuts each bean into four pieces.
4. Sets timer correctly.

Teaching Suggestions

- Ask the students which two characteristics or signs indicate that a liquid is boiling? (Answer: steam and bubbles.)

- Discuss and make a list of the types of food that can be boiled.

Green Beans — Serves 4

1 lb green beans · pot with lid · Italian dressing · colander · oven mitts · wooden spoon · knife · cutting board · 1 cup · Tablespoon

1 Rinse the green beans
2 Cut the ends off the green beans. Then cut each green bean into 4 pieces
3 Put 2 red cups water into the pot
4 Put the pot on the stove. Turn to **red**
5 Put the green beans into the pot
6 When the water boils
7 Put the lid on the pot. Turn to **blue**
8 Set the timer for 20 minutes
9 When the bell rings, turn to **white**
10 Put on oven mitts. Drain the green beans
11 Pour the green beans back into the pot
12 Add 2 red spoons Italian dressing
13 Stir and serve

2

32

Introduces concept of boiling. Green beans with Italian dressing is an alternative recipe to illustrate boiling.

Rice

Serves 6

1 Put 1 red cup rice in the pot

2 Put 2 red cups water in the pot

3 Put 1 red spoon butter in the pot

4 Add 1 blue spoon salt. Stir

5 Put the pot on the stove. Turn to **red**

6 When the water boils

7 Put the lid on the pot. Turn to **blue**.

8 Set the timer for 20 minutes.

9 When the bell rings, turn to **white**. Serve.

6

Recipe Narrative

Rice is a basic staple that can be enjoyed with a wide variety of main and side dishes. Both recipes are nutritious. Omit butter in rice recipe and dressing in green beans to reduce calories.

Lesson 14

Frying

Recipe:

Orange Pork Chop Skillet

Stress the importance of using a lid when frying.

Primary Objectives

1. Knows that frying means to cook food over high heat in a small amount of fat.
2. Recognizes what a frying pan is and knows that a nonstick frying pan is a good choice because it allows one to use less fat.
3. Recognizes and is able to safely operate a color-coded electric frying pan.

Secondary Objectives

1. Peels and slices orange.
2. Measures ingredients accurately.
3. Operates the color-coded stove.
4. Sets timer correctly.
5. Turns the pork chops over using the wooden spatula.
6. Stirs ingredients.

Teaching Suggestions

● Ask students to name their favorite fried foods. Discuss how a nonstick frying pan allows them to enjoy favorite fried foods while reducing calories.

● Demonstrate the color-coded nonstick electric frying pan. Put one red spoon of cooking oil and a pork chop in the pan and flip it: remove it from the pan and show students how it doesn't stick.

● Briefly demonstrate splattering and stress the importance of using a lid when frying anything.

● Discuss how spices and herbs can add interesting flavors to our foods. Demonstrate: let students sample a small piece of vegetable with and without spices.

● Present several different spices and herbs and see if the students can identify them by smell.

● Discuss and demonstrate how to trim fat from meat before it's cooked.

Introduces the concept of frying and emphasizes that a nonstick pan requires far less cooking fat and makes a far more healthy dish. (Note: Generally, one red spoon — 1 tablespoon — of fat will do.)

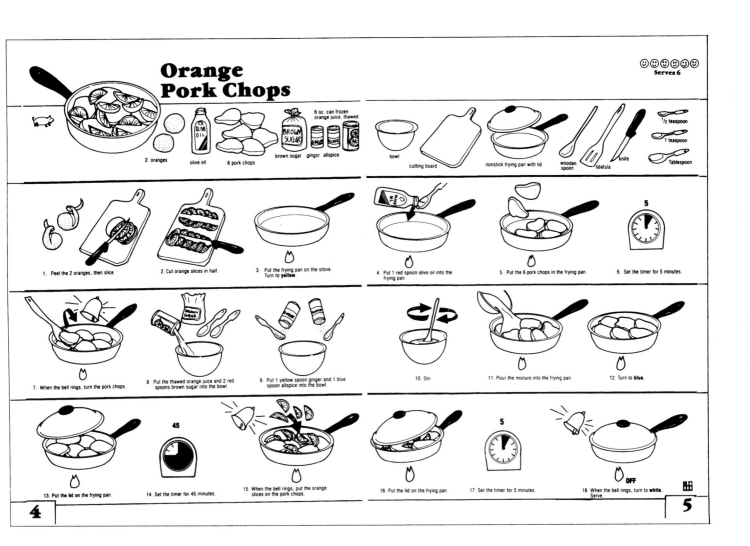

Orange Pork Chops

Serves 6

2 oranges · olive oil · 6 pork chops · brown sugar · ginger · allspice · 6 oz. can frozen orange juice, thawed

bowl · cutting board · nonstick frying pan with lid · wooden spoon · spatula · knife · 1/2 teaspoon · 1 teaspoon · Tablespoon

1. Peel the 2 oranges, then slice.
2. Cut orange slices in half.
3. Put the frying pan on the stove. Turn to **yellow**.
4. Put 1 red spoon olive oil into the frying pan.
5. Put the 6 pork chops in the frying pan.
6. Set the timer for 5 minutes.
7. When the bell rings, turn the pork chops.
8. Put the thawed orange juice and 2 red spoons brown sugar into the bowl.
9. Put 1 yellow spoon ginger and 1 blue spoon allspice into the bowl.
10. Stir.
11. Pour the mixture into the frying pan.
12. Turn to **blue**.
13. Put the lid on the frying pan.
14. Set the timer for 45 minutes.
15. When the bell rings, put the orange slices on the pork chops.
16. Put the lid on the frying pan.
17. Set the timer for 5 minutes.
18. When the bell rings, turn to **white**. Serve.

4   5

Recipe Narrative

This recipe makes a tasty and interesting pork chop. Rice and a green vegetable are nice side dishes. This is a good example of how herbs and spices can add flavor to basic foods.

35

Lesson 15

Baking

Recipe:
Baked Herb Chicken

Oven mitts must always be used when baking.

Primary Objectives

1. Knows that baking is the process of cooking some kinds of food uncovered in the oven.
2. Operates the oven by use of color-coded temperature settings.
3. Uses oven mitts consistently when putting something in or taking it out of the oven.

Secondary Objectives

1. Washes chicken before cooking it.
2. Measures ingredients accurately.
3. Sprinkles herbs, juice and spices over the entire surface of the chicken.

Teaching Suggestions

● Discuss with students the need to build up a small repertoire of healthy favorite foods, like chicken, hamburgers, fish, that can be prepared on a regular basis.

● Stress that oven mitts must always be used when putting something in or taking it out of the oven.

● Ask users to measure herbs. Hold a small amount in one palm, and scatter pinches over the entire surface of the chicken.

● Substitute or add other herbs for the suggested oregano. Use fresh minced garlic instead of garlic powder.

Introduces the concept of baking: the cooking of uncovered food in an oven. Students become familiar with baking equipment, like baking sheets and the square, round, loaf and rectangular pans made of metal or pyrex glass. Point out that glass pans can be used in both the conventional oven as well as in the microwave.

Herb Chicken

Serves 4

lemon juice   salt   pepper   oven mitts   ½ teaspoon

2 ½ lbs. chicken   garlic powder   oregano   2 ½ qt. baking dish   colander   1 teaspoon   Tablespoon

paprika

1. Preheat the oven. Turn to **yellow**
2. Wash the chicken
3. Arrange the chicken in a 2 ½ qt. baking dish

4. Sprinkle with 3 red spoons lemon juice, 1 blue spoon garlic powder and 1 yellow spoon paprika.
5. Sprinkle with 1 yellow spoon oregano, 1 blue spoon salt and 1 blue spoon pepper
6. Put on the oven mitts. Place the chicken in the oven.

55

7. Set the timer for 55 minutes.
8. When the bell rings, turn the oven to **white**
9. Put on the oven mitts. Remove the chicken from the oven. Serve

3

Recipe Narrative

This is a basic chicken recipe that is low in fat and calories, is simple to make yet flavorful and can easily become a part of the student's regular diet. To increase quantities, double the recipe and use a larger baking dish.

37

Lesson 16

Roasting

Recipe:

Roast Beef With Vegetables

Have students practice placing and removing roasting pan.

Primary Objectives

1. Knows that roasting means cooking meat or poultry uncovered in an oven. (Note: roasting differs from baking in that it usually involves cooking meat or poultry in large quantities, often whole.)
2. Knows that meat is usually placed on a rack in a shallow baking pan when roasted.

Secondary Objectives

1. Peels and cuts vegetables.
2. Operates color-coded oven.
3. Uses oven mitts.
4. Sets timer correctly.
5. Measures ingredients accurately.
6. Removes the roast beef from the oven and slices it.

Teaching Suggestions

● Practice placing and removing the shallow baking pan that is used in roasting meat or poultry. It can be somewhat heavy and bending over with a heavy item that's hot can be tricky. Simulate with water in a weighted pan.

● Stress the need for students to wear oven mitts at all times when taking something out of the oven.

● Emphasize to users that vegetables are an optional part of this recipe, but add greatly to it.

● Point out that other vegetables can be substituted, such as turnips.

Introduces the concept of roasting. Students learn that roasting, like baking, is food cooked uncovered in an oven.

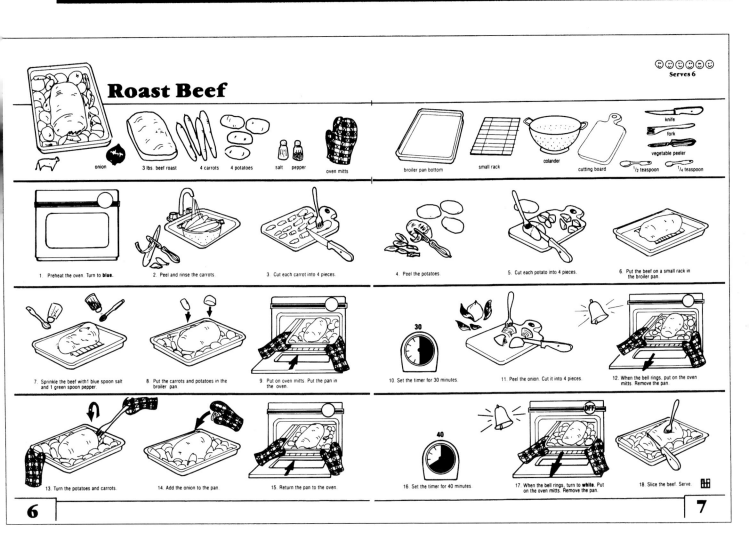

Roast Beef

Serves 6

onion | 3 lbs. beef roast | 4 carrots | 4 potatoes | salt | pepper | oven mitts | broiler pan bottom | small rack | colander | cutting board | knife | fork | vegetable peeler | 1/2 teaspoon | 1/4 teaspoon

1. Preheat the oven. Turn to **blue**.
2. Peel and rinse the carrots.
3. Cut each carrot into 4 pieces.
4. Peel the potatoes.
5. Cut each potato into 4 pieces.
6. Put the beef on a small rack in the broiler pan.
7. Sprinkle the beef with 1 blue spoon salt and 1 green spoon pepper.
8. Put the carrots and potatoes in the broiler pan.
9. Put on oven mitts. Put the pan in the oven.
10. Set the timer for 30 minutes.
11. Peel the onion. Cut it into 4 pieces.
12. When the bell rings, put on the oven mitts. Remove the pan.
13. Turn the potatoes and carrots.
14. Add the onion to the pan.
15. Return the pan to the oven.
16. Set the timer for 40 minutes.
17. When the bell rings, turn to **white**. Put on the oven mitts. Remove the pan.
18. Slice the beef. Serve.

6   7

Recipe Narrative

By simply adding vegetables to the roasting pan this dish becomes a full meal. It tastes great and can feed a crowd. A smaller roast can be prepared but roasting time must be proportionally reduced.

Lesson 17

Broiling

Recipe:

Broiled Fish Filets

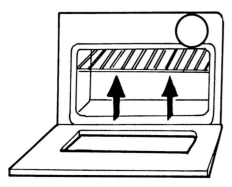

Adjust the rack to high level.

Primary Objectives

1. Knows that broiling means cooking food by direct heat on a rack.
2. Knows that most stoves come with a broiling pan that consists of a rack and a pan.
3. Knows that broiling is a healthy method of cooking because little if any fat is used.
4. Operates the broiler.

Secondary Objectives

1. Measures ingredients accurately.
2. Uses oven mitts when using the broiler.
3. Sets timer correctly.

Teaching Suggestions

- Practice turning the broiler on and off and point out that the color for turning it on is green.
- Discuss what broiling means. Introduce the component parts of a broiler: pan and rack, and stress that they must always be used together. Note that the pan can be used with a smaller rack when roasting meats.
- Cooks can substitute their own dressing for that called for in the recipe. Mix a little olive oil with thyme, tarragon or oregano and a little bit of lemon juice.

Introduces the concept of broiling. Students learn that broiled foods are cooked quickly by direct heat on a rack.

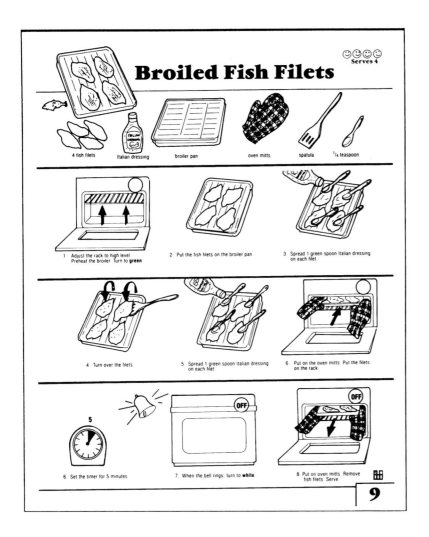

Broiled Fish Filets

Serves 4

| 4 fish filets | Italian dressing | broiler pan | oven mitts | spatula | ¼ teaspoon |

1 Adjust the rack to high level. Preheat the broiler. Turn to **green**

2 Put the fish filets on the broiler pan

3 Spread 1 green spoon Italian dressing on each filet

4 Turn over the filets

5 Spread 1 green spoon Italian dressing on each filet

6 Put on the oven mitts. Put the filets on the rack

6 Set the timer for 5 minutes

7 When the bell rings, turn to **white**

8 Put on oven mitts. Remove fish filets. Serve

9

Recipe Narrative

This is a simple, tasty and nutritious recipe for fish filets.

41

Making Meals

Recipes:

Orange Pork Chop Skillet

Rice

Green Beans

Primary Objectives

1. Prepares a series of recipes simultaneously or in order from the one that takes the most to the one that takes the least amount of time.
2. Follows the Meal Plan presented below.
3. Operates two timers—a hand-held one and the built-in stove timer or two hand-held ones.

Meal Plan—Simultaneously

1. Prepare the orange pork chop skillet recipe through step #14. Puts the timer on the pork chop recipe page.
2. Prepare the green beans with Italian dressing (or olive oil) recipe through step #8. Puts the timer on the green beans recipe page.
3. Prepare the rice in its entirety, putting timer on rice recipe page. If a third timer is unavailable, watch the clock for 20 minutes.
4. Finish the green beans recipe but leave in pan or put into covered server to keep warm.
5. Finish the pork chop recipe by adding the orange slices and cooking for five more minutes.
6. Serve the meal.

Meal Plan—In Order

1. Orange pork chop skillet
2. Rice
3. Green beans with Italian dressing

Orange Pork Chops with Rice and Green Beans

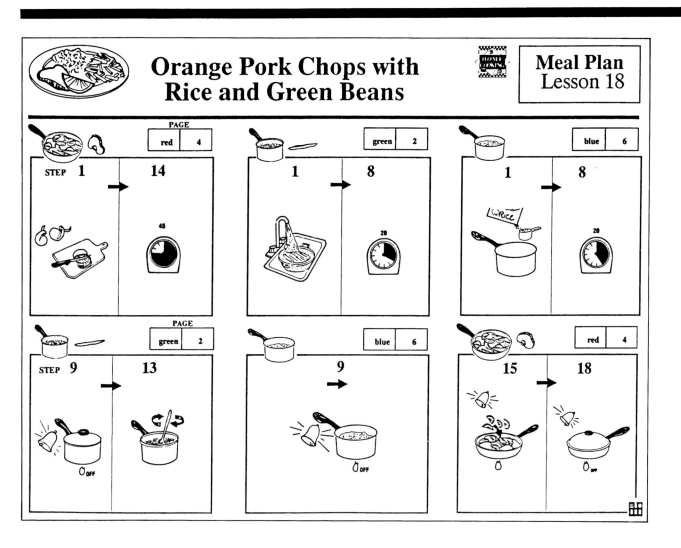

Food Varieties

Fresh Foods

Recipe:

Corn on the Cob

Stress washing fresh foods before eating them.

Primary Objectives

1. Knows most fresh foods, including meats, dairy products, fruits and vegetables are stored in the refrigerator.
2. Knows most fresh foods are wrapped or stored in containers while refrigerated.
3. Recognizes spoiled food and discards it.
4. Washes poultry, fruits and vegetables before cooking or eating them.

Secondary Objectives

1. Husks corn.
2. Operates color-coded stove.
3. Uses tongs to pick up corn.
4. Sets timer correctly.
5. Recognizes boiling water.

Teaching Suggestions

- Discuss that some foods, such as corn, come in different varieties. Ask students to name three varieties of corn and where is each stored. Q: Fresh? A: Refrigerator. Q: Canned? A: Cupboard. Q: Frozen? A: Freezer.
  Focus on fresh corn and discuss why it tastes best if stored in the refrigerator and used as soon as possible. (Note: Ideally it will used the same day as purchased.)

- Q: Ask students what signs indicate that food has spoiled. A: It smells different. A: There might be mold. A: A change in appearance. Q: What happens if you eat spoiled food? A: You might get very sick.

- Explain that some packaged foods, such as meats, breads and dairy products have expiration dates and instruct students to check dates. Discuss why they shouldn't purchase foods with expired dates because they will spoil too quickly.

- Practice putting fresh foods away, including wrapping with plastic and sealing in containers.

Introduces concept of buying and storing fresh foods. Freshness is a factor that impacts the selection and the shelf life of many foods.

- Have students wash fresh fruits and vegetables as soon as they return from shopping to clean off sprays, dirt or bacteria.

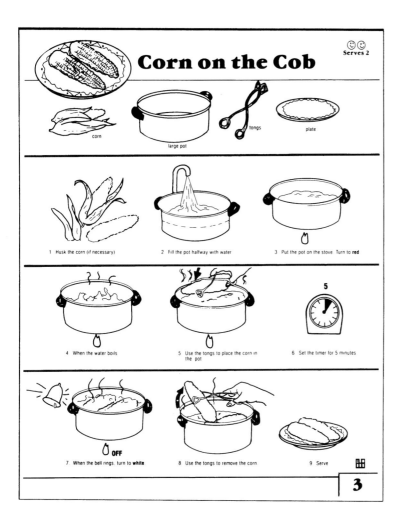

Recipe Narrative

Corn on the cob is a favorite vegetable of many people and it provides a good example of how to buy and store fresh foods.

Lesson 20

Canned Foods

Recipe:

*Tuna Salad
Sandwich*

*Have students practice
using can openers.*

Primary Objectives

1. Puts canned foods in cupboards.
2. Operates a hand-held or electric can opener.
3. Transfers leftover canned foods to a glass or plastic container and stores in the refrigerator.
4. Knows canned foods come in different sizes and uses the correct size as stated in a given recipe.

Secondary Objectives

1. Washes fresh vegetables before using them.
2. Chops vegetables using a knife, fork and cutting board.
3. Places the colander in the sink when draining liquids.
4. Stirs ingredients.
5. Spreads food evenly on a slice of bread.

Teaching Suggestions

● Discuss different ways in which the same foods are packaged, such as beans, which are available fresh, frozen or canned. Point out that meat, fish, chicken, fruits and some dairy products also come in different forms. Focus on canned goods and ask students to name some foods that come in cans.

● Point out the differences in can sizes. Note that students should key off recipes for the correct size desired, or by the number of people being served.

● Discuss storage. Stock unopened cans in cupboards and transfer leftovers from cans to storage containers and put in refrigerator or freezer.

● Practice using hand-held and electric can openers.

● Have users make a chart showing the ways in which one kind of food can be packaged. Clip food pictures from magazines and place next to a picture of its storage place: e.g., fresh beans in refrigerator, frozen in freezer and canned on shelves.

Introduces the use of canned foods, including storage, size discrimination and operating hand-held, wall mounted or electric can openers.

Tuna Salad Sandwich

Serves 3

celery stalk, colander, bowl, ¼ teaspoon, Tablespoon, ⅓ cup, pepper, tuna, mayonnaise, onion, fork, knife, can opener, cutting board, bread

1. Rinse the celery.
2. Cut the celery into small pieces.
3. Peel the onion.
4. Chop 1 red spoon onion.
5. Open the tuna. Pour it into the colander and drain.
6. Pour the tuna into the bowl. Break the tuna into small pieces.
7. Add the celery and red spoon onion.
8. Add 1 blue cup lite mayonnaise and 1 green spoon pepper.
9. Stir.
10. Spread 1 blue cup tuna on a slice of bread.
11. Put another piece of bread on top to make a sandwich. Serve.

8

Recipe Narrative

This tuna salad recipe is low in fat and calories because it is prepared with vegetables and lite mayonnaise. An alternative would be to use regular mayonnaise and no vegetables.

Lesson 21

Frozen Foods

Recipe:

Frozen Strawberry Drink

or Succotash

Primary Objectives

1. Puts frozen foods in a freezer.
2. Finds adequate containers for food that goes in the freezer.
3. Knows certain foods, such as meats, fruits and vegetables can be kept longer in a freezer than in a refrigerator.

Secondary Objectives

1. Measures ingredients accurately using color-coded cups and spoons.
2. Uses a blender.
3. Operates a color-coded stove.
4. Recognizes boiling water.
5. Sets timer correctly.
6. Stirs ingredients.

Teaching Suggestions

- Show frozen strawberries or frozen corn and lima beans to students.
  Q: What do they feel? A: Hardness and coldness.
  Q: Where are frozen foods stored? A: In the freezer.
- Present a variety of freezer containers and wrapping materials and discuss how to store foods that need to be frozen.
- Explain the difference between freezer and refrigerator storage times: e.g., strawberries will last a few days in the refrigerator but up to a year in the freezer.

Introduces the use of frozen foods. Students understand that frozen foods must remain frozen until they are prepared.

Recipe Narrative

Frozen strawberry drink is a delicious dessert that is low in fat, cholesterol and calories. For a thicker shake add more frozen strawberries. The succotash recipe shows how two frozen vegetables combine to make a new dish.

Leftovers

Recipe:

Chicken Soup

*Chicken Soup is usually made with
leftovers in mind.*

Primary Objectives

1. Decides where a leftover is stored based on how quickly it will be used. Short-term is defined as within 72 hours and requires refrigeration. Freeze anything to be stored for over three days.
2. Stores leftovers in covered containers or wrapping, like foil, plastic wrap or freezer paper.
3. Prepares and freezes in advance recipes that take a long time to make. These can include soup, spaghetti sauce and meatballs, and can be made in large quantities to be reheated in microwave or stove.

Secondary Objectives

1. Slices vegetables carefully.
2. Measures ingredients accurately using color-coded cups and spoons.
3. Operates color-coded stove.
4. Sets timer correctly.
5. Recognizes boiling.
6. Rinses chicken and vegetables before using.
7. Stirs ingredients.

Teaching Suggestions

● Explain and discuss the reasons why making some recipes in large quantities in advance is a good idea. (Because they take a long time to prepare and they freeze and reheat well.) Demonstrate. Make, freeze and reheat meatballs, or sauce with the class.

● Discuss freezing and refrigerating storage methods.
Q: What type of containers and wrapping should be used for freezing? A: Airtight.
Q: How about refrigerator leftovers? A: They should be covered but not as tightly.

● Discuss length of storage time: as a general rule, freeze anything that needs to last more than 72 hours.

Introduces the concept of leftover storage. Students learn to decide when to refrigerate and when to freeze. Also suggests the idea of preparing and some recipes, like chicken soup, in large quantities and freezing portions for later use.

Chicken Soup

Serves 8

2 lbs chicken pieces   4 carrots   onion   2 celery stalks   chicken bouillon   pepper   salt   large pot with lid   colander   cutting board   knife   fork   peeler   wooden spoon   ladle   1 cup   Tablespoon   1 teaspoon   ¼ teaspoon

1 Rinse the chicken
2 Put the chicken into the pot
3 Rinse the carrots and celery
4 Peel and slice the carrots
5 Slice the celery
6 Peel and slice the onion
7 Put the carrots, celery and onions into the pot
8 Add 4 red cups water
9 Add 1 yellow spoon salt and 1 green spoon pepper
10 Add 1 red spoon chicken bouillon
11 Stir
12 Put the pot on the stove. Turn to **red**
13 When the soup begins to boil
14 Put the lid on the pot. Turn to **blue**
15 Set the timer for 55 minutes
16 When the bell rings, turn to **white**
17 Serve

10   11

Recipe Narrative

This recipe introduces homemade soup. It can be doubled without increasing the amount of chicken. Other vegetables can be substituted.

51

Making Meals

Recipes:

Fish Filet

Succotash

Primary Objectives

1. Prepares a series of recipes simultaneously or in order starting with the one that takes the most to the one that takes the least amount of time.
2. Follows the Meal Plan successfully.

Meal Plan—Simultaneously

1. Begin succotash and prepare through step #8.
2. Begin the fish filets recipe and prepare through step #5.
3. Complete succotash recipe when the bell rings.
4. Resume fish filets recipe on step #6 and complete.
5. Serve the meal.

Meal Plan—In Order

1. Prepare the succotash.
2. Prepare the fish filets.
3. Serve the meal.

Fish Filets with Succotash

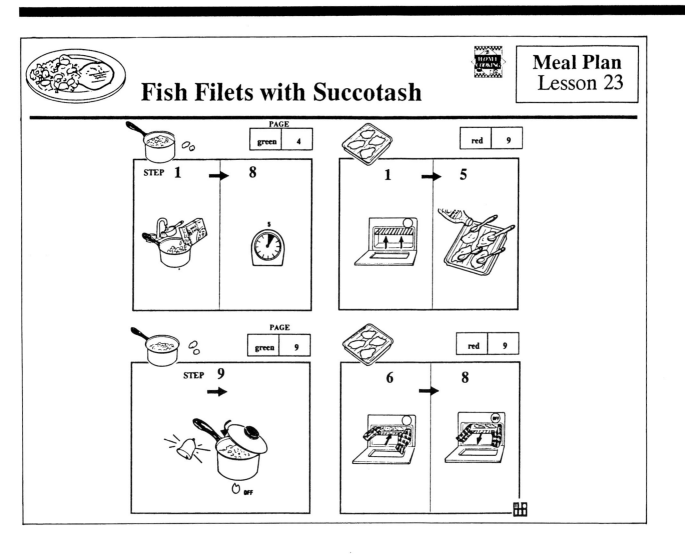

53

Making Meals

Recipes:

Tuna Salad Sandwich

Corn on the Cob

Primary Objectives

1. Prepares a series of recipes in order from the one that takes the most to the one that takes the least amount of time.
2. Follows the steps for each recipe presented in the cookbook.

Meal Plan

1. Prepare tuna salad through step #9 and refrigerate.
2. Prepare corn on the cob.
3. Remove tuna from refrigerator and do steps #10 and 11.
4. Serve the meal.

Tuna Salad Sandwich with Corn on the Cob

Meal Plan
Lesson 24

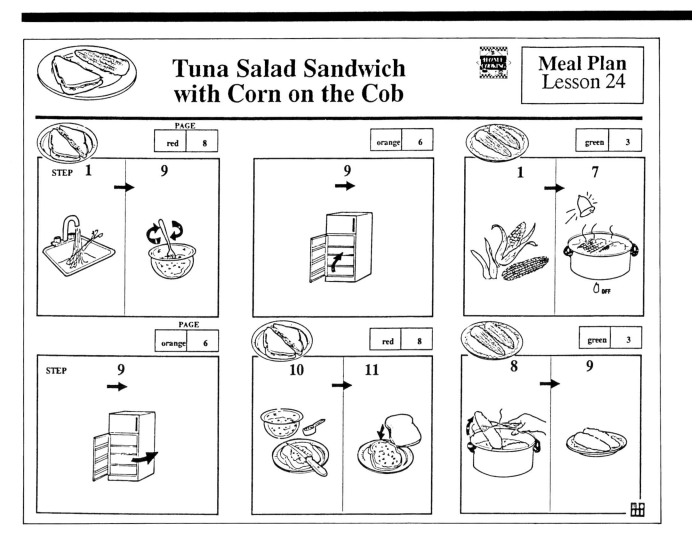

Microwave Cooking

Color-coded Microwave Oven

Recipe:

Microwave Baked Potatoes

or Microwave Bacon (Supplemental Recipe)

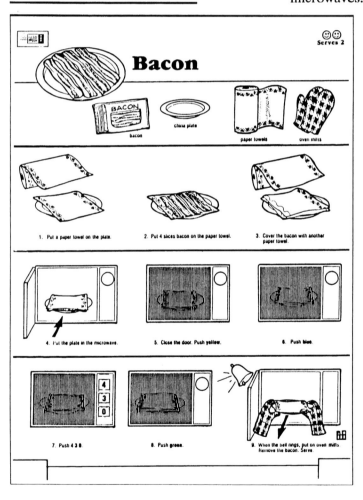

Primary Objectives

1. Operates the color-coded microwave oven.
2. Places food item on a paper towel in the microwave.
3. Uses oven mitts to remove food from the microwave.
4. Recognizes the microwave logo when it appears on Home Cooking recipes.
5. Understands that metal pans and foil wrap are unsuitable for microwaves.

Secondary Objectives

1. Washes potatoes.
2. Pricks potatoes with a fork to allow steam to escape.

Teaching Suggestions

● Q: Ask how many students have a microwave oven. Q: Ask how many have ever used one.

● Present the color-coded microwave oven to the students together with the recipe for microwave baked potatoes. Orient them to color and number buttons and have users practice.

● Caution students never to start an empty oven. Users can practice turning it on and off and making time settings by placing a cup of water inside.

● Emphasize the need to use oven mitts as a precaution.

Introduces the use of microwave oven. Like the stove, the microwave is color-coded to designate temperature settings and cooking time.

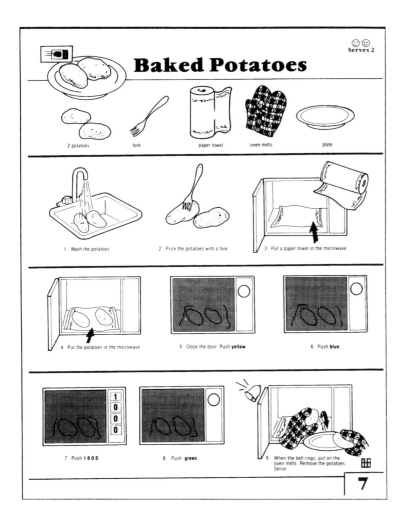

Baked Potatoes

Serves 2

2 potatoes | fork | paper towel | oven mitts | plate

1. Wash the potatoes
2. Prick the potatoes with a fork
3. Put a paper towel in the microwave
4. Put the potatoes in the microwave
5. Close the door. Push **yellow**
6. Push **blue**.
7. Push **1 0 0 0**.
8. Push **green**.
9. When the bell rings, put on the oven mitts. Remove the potatoes. Serve

7

Recipe Narrative

If you are using a microwave to bake potatoes, consider the time factor involved: one potato cooks in six minutes, three cook in 15 minutes and four take 20 minutes. If you are cooking more than four, it's better to use a conventional oven.

Lesson 26

Plastic Wrap/Wax Paper

Recipe:

Microwave Vegetable Platter

Primary Objectives

1. Operates color-coded microwave oven.
2. Understands the importance of arranging food on the platter to maximize cooking time as stated in recipe.
3. Covers plate tightly with plastic wrap so vegetables can steam.
4. Uses oven mitts when removing food from microwave.
5. Slits plastic before removing it to allow steam to escape.

Secondary Objectives

1. Uses a knife, fork and cutting board to cut vegetables.
2. Uses a vegetable peeler.
3. Measures ingredients accurately.
4. Washes peeled vegetables.

Teaching Suggestions

- Review microwave color-coding.
- Explain that foods are specially positioned because microwave heat radiates in toward the center, cooking peripheral items faster than those placed in the middle of the dish.
- Demonstrate platter placements: slow cooking parts, like vegetable stems, face outward, while fast cooking parts should be in the center of the plate.
- Show how steaming works by example: cover a vegetable plate with plastic wrap and follow the recipe.
- Use wax paper to cover foods to reduce splatter.
- Some microwave dishes need to be turned over or the plate rotated to cook evenly. Discuss and demonstrate.

■ 58

Introduces the use of plastic wrap and wax paper as coverings when cooking with a microwave oven. Paper or plastic coverings, with a minimum of water on the platter, make it possible to steam vegetables, a cooking method that preserves nutritional value.

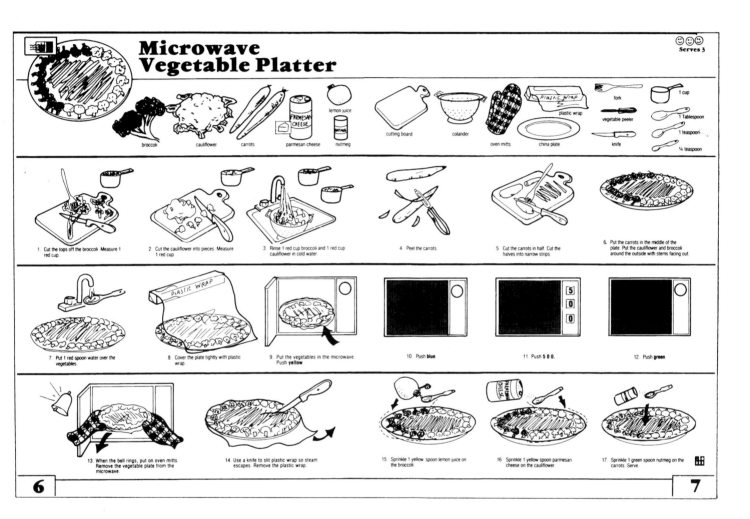

Microwave Vegetable Platter

Serves 3

broccoli — cauliflower — carrots — parmesan cheese — nutmeg — lemon juice — cutting board — colander — oven mitts — plastic wrap — china plate — fork — vegetable peeler — knife — 1 cup — 1 Tablespoon — 1 teaspoon — ¼ teaspoon

1. Cut the tops off the broccoli. Measure 1 red cup.
2. Cut the cauliflower into pieces. Measure 1 red cup.
3. Rinse 1 red cup broccoli and 1 red cup cauliflower in cold water.
4. Peel the carrots.
5. Cut the carrots in half. Cut the halves into narrow strips.
6. Put the carrots in the middle of the plate. Put the cauliflower and broccoli around the outside with stems facing out.
7. Put 1 red spoon water over the vegetables.
8. Cover the plate tightly with plastic wrap.
9. Put the vegetables in the microwave. Push **yellow**.
10. Push **blue**.
11. Push **5 0 0**.
12. Push **green**.
13. When the bell rings, put on oven mitts. Remove the vegetable plate from the microwave.
14. Use a knife to slit plastic wrap so steam escapes. Remove the plastic wrap.
15. Sprinkle 1 yellow spoon lemon juice on the broccoli.
16. Sprinkle 1 yellow spoon parmesan cheese on the cauliflower.
17. Sprinkle 1 green spoon nutmeg on the carrots. Serve.

6   7

Recipe Narrative

This is a healthy and tasty treat that is simple and quick to make. The toppings provide a diversity of flavors yet the dish remains low in fat, salt and calories.

59

Lesson 27

Defrosting & Reheating

Recipe:

*Microwave
Barbecued Chicken*

Primary Objectives

1. Uses the microwave to defrost foods on 30% or 3 power.
2. Reheats leftovers in the microwave, covered either with plastic wrap (tightly) or wax paper (loosely).
3. Operates the color-coded microwave.

Secondary Objectives

1. Measures ingredients accurately using color-coded cups and spoons.
2. Stirs ingredients.

Teaching Suggestions

- Discuss and demonstrate: microwaves are a good way to defrost frozen foods. There are different names or numbers for the defrost cycle, depending on your unit. Some defrost cycles are 30%, some are 3, some medium-low. (Note: defrosting chicken for this recipe takes from 25-30 minutes.)
- Caution: always cook meat immediately after defrosting it in the microwave oven to avoid spoilage.
- Explain that microwaves are also great for reheating last night's leftovers which have been refrigerated, as well as frozen leftovers from last week. When reheating leftovers cover tightly with plastic wrap so they won't dry out. The exception is baked goods: wrap them tightly in microwave-safe paper toweling. Use 100% power for short periods of time, e.g. 30 seconds. Soups and sauces, covered tightly take 4-5 minutes to heat to boiling.

60

Introduces the use of the microwave to defrost and reheat many types of food and leftovers. This is one of its handiest uses because it is fast and mess free: reheated leftovers don't stick to containers making it easy to clean up.

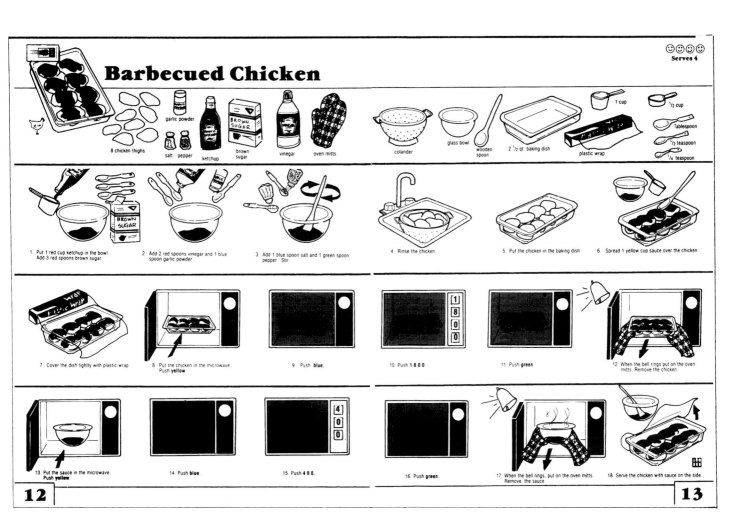

Barbecued Chicken

Serves 4

garlic powder

8 chicken thighs salt pepper ketchup brown sugar vinegar oven mitts

colander glass bowl wooden spoon 2 1/2 qt. baking dish plastic wrap

1 cup 1/2 cup Tablespoon 1/2 teaspoon 1/4 teaspoon

1. Put 1 red cup ketchup in the bowl. Add 3 red spoons brown sugar.

2. Add 2 red spoons vinegar and 1 blue spoon garlic powder.

3. Add 1 blue spoon salt and 1 green spoon pepper. Stir.

4. Rinse the chicken.

5. Put the chicken in the baking dish.

6. Spread 1 yellow cup sauce over the chicken.

7. Cover the dish tightly with plastic wrap.

8. Put the chicken in the microwave. Push **yellow**

9. Push **blue**.

10. Push **1 8 0 0**

11. Push **green**

12. When the bell rings put on the oven mitts. Remove the chicken.

13. Put the sauce in the microwave. Push **yellow**.

14. Push **blue**.

15. Push **4 0 0**.

16. Push **green**.

17. When the bell rings, put on the oven mitts. Remove the sauce.

18. Serve the chicken with sauce on the side.

12 | | 13

Recipe Narrative

This recipe is a simple and quick but delicious way to prepare chicken. It takes advantage of the best features of microwave cooking, which are speed and efficiency.

61

Lesson 28
Special Dishes For Microwave

Recipes:

Microwave
Meat Loaf

or Microwave
Fish Filets
(Supplemental Recipe)

Primary Objectives

1. Operates color-coded microwave.
2. Knows which containers and wraps can be used in a microwave, like glass, china, plastic, paper.
3. Knows not to put metal items in microwaves.

Secondary Objectives

1. Measures ingredients accurately using color-coded cups and spoons.
2. Cuts and chops onion.
3. Stirs ingredients.
4. Sets timer.
5. Uses oven mitts to remove food.

Teaching Suggestions

● Present different types of containers and wraps to the students and ask which ones are safe for use in the microwave oven. Correct answers for safe are: glass, ceramic, china (without silver or gold trim), paper, plastic (with microwave seal), microwave plastic wrap, wax paper and paper towels.

● Ask which are not safe. Correct answers for unsafe are: metal pans and dishes.

● Discuss: some materials such as paper plates, china dishes and some plastic containers are good for reheating small quantities but not for larger amounts. Oven-proof glass dishes are more versatile and can be used in microwaves and stoves and are recommended for use with Home Cooking microwave recipes.

● Microwave plastic wraps make a tight seal and keep the steam in for even cooking. Pierce plastic with a knife after cooking to vent steam. Caution students to do this only with oven mitts on.

Introduces the concept of cooking a main dish in a microwave.
Choose either the fish filet or meat loaf recipe.

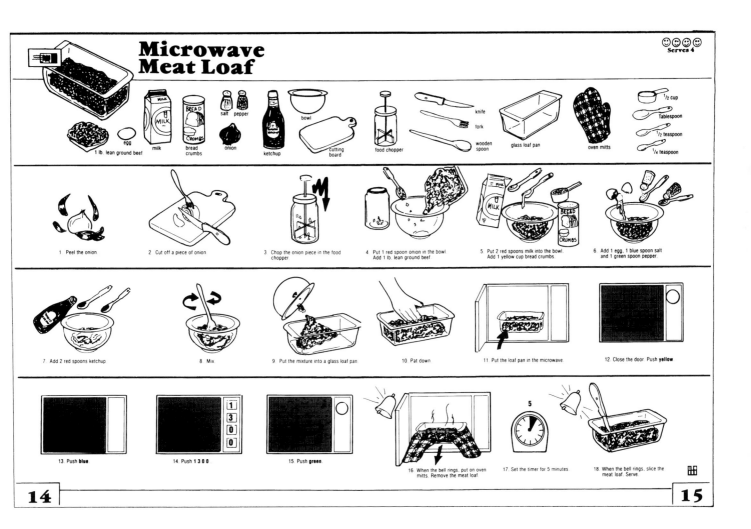

Microwave Meat Loaf

Serves 4

1 lb. lean ground beef / egg / milk / salt / pepper / bread crumbs / onion / ketchup / bowl / Cutting board / food chopper / knife / fork / wooden spoon / glass loaf pan / oven mitts / ½ cup / Tablespoon / ½ teaspoon / ¼ teaspoon

1. Peel the onion.
2. Cut off a piece of onion.
3. Chop the onion piece in the food chopper.
4. Put 1 red spoon onion in the bowl. Add 1 lb. lean ground beef.
5. Put 2 red spoons milk into the bowl. Add 1 yellow cup bread crumbs.
6. Add 1 egg. 1 blue spoon salt and 1 green spoon pepper.
7. Add 2 red spoons ketchup.
8. Mix.
9. Put the mixture into a glass loaf pan.
10. Pat down.
11. Put the loaf pan in the microwave.
12. Close the door. Push **yellow**.
13. Push **blue**.
14. Push **1 3 0 0**.
15. Push **green**.
16. When the bell rings. put on oven mitts. Remove the meat loaf.
17. Set the timer for 5 minutes.
18. When the bell rings, slice the meat loaf. Serve.

14   15

Recipe Narrative

This is a quick and easy recipe for meat loaf that browns nicely in the microwave because of the fat content in the meat.

63

Lesson 29

Making Microwave Meals

Recipe:

*Microwave
Meat Loaf*

Baked Potatoes

---

*Microwave
Vegetable Platter*

Note: If you are preparing the recipes one at a time, follow the above order.

Primary Objectives

1. Prepares a series of recipes simultaneously.
2. Follows recipe Meal Plan.

Meal Plan—Simultaneously

1. Prepare the meat loaf through step #15.
2. Prepare the vegetable platter through step #8.
3. Prepare the baked potatoes through step #2.
4. Do step #16, meat loaf.
5. Finish the baked potatoe recipe while the meat loaf is cooling.
6. When the potatoes are done, place in covered container and continue with step #9 of the vegetable platter, until completion.
7. Serve the meal.

Meat Loaf with Baked Potato and Vegetable Platter

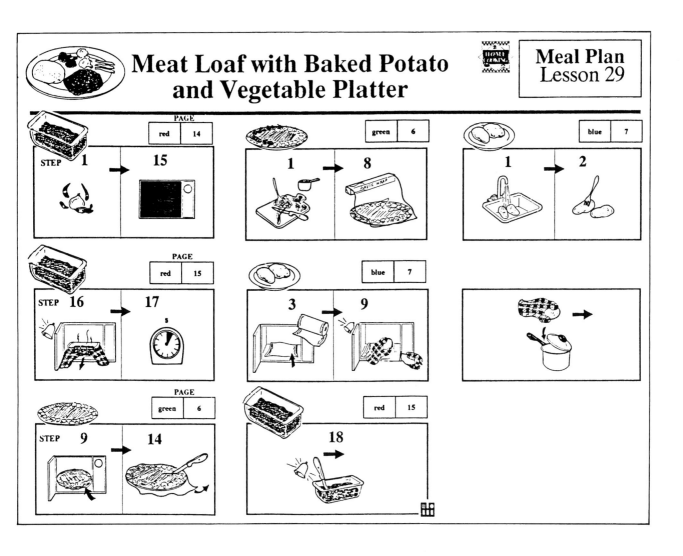

Lesson 30

Making Microwave Meals

Recipe

*Microwave
Potato Salad*

---

*Microwave
Barbecued Chicken*

Microwave Asparagus

Note: If preparing the recipes one at a time, follow the above order.

Primary Objectives

1. Prepares a series of recipes simultaneously or in order from the one that takes the most to the one that takes the least amount of time.
2. Knows preparing some recipes in advance saves time.
3. Follows Meal Plan successfully.

Meal Plan—Simultaneously

1. Prepare potato salad and refrigerate.
2. Prepare barbecued chicken through step #11.
3. Prepare asparagus through step #4.
4. When the bell rings, remove the chicken (step #12) and continue with asparagus from step #5 to its conclusion.
5. Continue barbecued chicken recipe from step #13 to its conclusion.
6. Serve the meal.

66

BBQ Chicken with Asparagus and Potato Salad

Menu Planning

Nutrition

Recipe:

Chili

Primary Objectives

1. Knows the four food groups: milk, meat, vegetables and fruit, bread and cereal.
2. Understands a balanced diet is eating from all four groups every day.
3. Knows the difference between nutritious foods, found in the four food groups, and junk foods, high in fats, sugar and empty calories.

Secondary Objectives

1. Operates color-coded stove.
2. Rinses vegetables before using them.
3. Chops vegetables.
4. Measures ingredients accurately using color-coded cups and spoons.
5. Stirs ingredients.
6. Sets timer.

Teaching Suggestions

- Show students a chart of the four food groups: ask them to name the groups and the foods found in each one.

- Discuss the importance of choosing a variety of foods for the sake of good health: milk group—3-4 servings for children, 2 for adults; meat group—2 servings; fruit and vegetable group—4 servings; bread and cereal group—4 servings.

- Ask students to name some junk foods, such as soda, cookies, candy, cakes, pies, chips. Ask them to name some nutritious foods, such as meats, vegetables, fruits, breads, cereals and dairy products.

- Demonstrate: have students plan a nutritious meal by choosing an item from each group.

Introduces the subject of nutrition and the need to eat daily from each of the four food groups.

Chili

Serves 5

1 lb. ground round | green pepper | onion | 16 oz. can tomatoes | 15 oz. can kidney beans | salt | pepper | chili powder | cumin | garlic powder | cutting board | frying pan with lid | colander | food chopper | can opener | knife | wooden spoon | Tablespoon | 1 teaspoon | 1/2 teaspoon | 1/4 teaspoon

1. Rinse the green pepper
2. Chop the green pepper
3. Peel and chop the onion
4. Put the frying pan on the stove. Turn to **yellow**.
5. Put the green pepper and onion into the pan. Add the ground round
6. Stir
7. Set the timer for 10 minutes
8. When the bell rings, open and add the can of tomatoes and 1 blue spoon garlic powder
9. Add 2 red spoons chili powder and 1 yellow spoon cumin
10. Add 1 green spoon pepper and and 1 yellow spoon salt
11. Stir
12. Put the lid on the pan. Turn to **blue**
13. Set the timer for 55 minutes
14. Open and drain the kidney beans
15. When the bell rings, add the kidney beans
16. Stir
17. Set the timer for 15 minutes
18. When the bell rings turn to **white**. Serve

16   17

Recipe Narrative

The chili recipe is a good example of a popular and common food that contains a member in good standing from each of the four food groups. Bread and milk or cheese can be used as side dishes to include all groups. To lower fat and calorie content, substitute ground turkey for lean ground beef.

Low Fat and Low Salt Diets

Recipe:

Vegetable Soup

or Tuna Salad Sandwich

Tuna Salad Sandwich
Serves 3

celery stalk

pepper · tuna · mayonnaise · onion · fork · knife · colander · bowl · ¼ teaspoon · Tablespoon · can opener · cutting board · bread · ⅓ cup

1. Rinse the celery.
2. Cut the celery into small pieces.
3. Peel the onion.
4. Chop 1 red spoon onion.
5. Open the tuna. Pour it into the colander and drain.
6. Pour the tuna into the bowl. Break the tuna into small pieces.
7. Add the celery and 1 spoon onion.
8. Add 1 blue cup lite mayonnaise and 1 green spoon pepper.
9. Stir.
10. Spread 1 blue cup tuna on a slice of bread.
11. Put another piece of bread on top to make a sandwich. Serve.

8

Primary Objectives

1. Uses herbs and spices to enhance flavor of foods instead of large amounts of salt.
2. Uses low fat mayonnaise, skim milk and yogurt in place of their higher fat counterparts, if desired.

Secondary Objectives

1. Washes vegetables before using them.
2. Pares carrots.
3. Chops vegetables using knife, fork and cutting board or food chopper.
4. Accurately measures ingredients using color-coded cups and spoons.
5. Sautes vegetables.
6. Sets timer.
7. Operates color-coded stove.
8. Mixes ingredients.
9. Spreads on bread. (If doing tuna sandwich.)

Teaching Suggestions

- Discuss: healthy diets are low in fats and salt; herbs and spices are good salt substitutes; low fat mayonnaise, yogurt, skim milk and low fat cheeses are better choices than their counterparts.
- Instruct students to do the following match:

Low Fat	Higher Fat
light mayonnaise	mayonnaise
skim milk	sour cream
yogurt	whole milk
cottage cheese	cheddar, cream cheese
part-skim mozzarella	ice cream
part-skim ricotta	
ice milk, frozen yogurt	

Introduces the concept of cooking for low salt diets. This is a concern for some on special diets, and a more general concern for all of us: how to enjoy flavorful food without oversalting.

Vegetable Soup

Serves 8

2 small zucchinis · onion · 2 carrots · 2 celery stalks · ½ lb. green beans · two 17 oz. cans tomatoes · olive oil · two 16 oz. cans chicken broth · parsley · pepper · basil · oregano · garlic powder · large pot · cutting board · colander · food chopper · fork · knife · vegetable peeler · ladle · wooden spoon · Tablespoon · 1 teaspoon · ¼ teaspoon

1. Wash the carrots, celery, green beans and zucchini.
2. Peel the carrots. Chop the carrots.
3. Chop the celery.
4. Peel the onion. Chop the onion.
5. Put the large pot on the stove. Turn to **yellow**.
6. Put 2 red spoons olive oil into the pot.
7. Add the carrots, celery and onion. Stir.
8. Set the timer for 5 minutes.
9. When the bell rings, open and add 2 cans tomatoes and 1 green spoon pepper.
10. Add 1 yellow spoon basil, 1 yellow spoon oregano and 1 yellow spoon garlic powder. Stir.
11. Set the timer for 15 minutes.
12. Cut off the ends of the green beans. Cut the beans into 4 pieces.
13. When the bell rings, open and add 2 cans chicken broth. Add the green beans.
14. Set the timer for 30 minutes.
15. Slice the zucchini.
16. When the bell rings, add the zucchini and 1 red spoon parsley.
17. Stir.
18. Turn to **white**. Serve.

18   19

Recipe Narrative

This vegetable soup recipe is a good example of a delicious dish low in salt and fat. It also freezes well.

71

Lesson 33

Textures and Colors

Recipe:

Spinach Salad

Salads offer an appealing mixture of textures and colors.

Primary Objectives

1. Plans menus with foods of different colors and understands why a meal should be visually appealing.
2. Plans meals that include a variety of food textures and understands that is important.

Secondary Objectives

1. Washes vegetables before using them.
2. Slices vegetables using knife, fork and cutting board.
3. Accurately measures ingredients using color-coded cups and spoons.
4. Beats ingredients with a fork.
5. Stirs ingredients.

Teaching Suggestions

● Present the following menu and ask the students if they find it appealing.

        Broiled Fish Filets
        Mashed Potatoes
        Cauliflower
        Vanilla Pudding

Q: What's wrong with this picture from a visual standpoint?
A: All the foods are white and soft.
Q: How can you improve this menu?
A: Substitute foods that provide variety of color and texture.
For example:

        Broiled Fish Filets
        Carrots with Nutmeg
        Spinach Salad
        Chocolate Chip Cookies

● Stress the importance of using different colors and different textures when planning a menu.

Introduces the concept of visually appealing meals. Part of the appeal of food is the way it looks. This lesson deals with a visual orientation to meal preparation.

● Chopped or sliced hard boiled eggs and bacon bits can be added for more color and flavor.

Recipe Narrative

This recipe features contrasting colors, white and green, and textures, crisp and soft.

Breakfast

Recipe:

Scrambled Eggs and Pancakes
(Supplemental Recipes)

---

or Scrambled Eggs
(Supplemental Recipe)
and Biscuits

Primary Objectives

1. Prepares a series of recipes from the one that takes the longest to the one that takes the shortest amount of time.
2. Puts together a nutritious breakfast menu.

Secondary Objectives

1. Operates color-coded stove and oven.
2. Measures ingredients accurately using color-coded cups and spoons.
3. Sets timer.
4. Kneads dough.
5. Rolls out dough.
6. Uses oven mitts when putting biscuits in or taking them out of the oven.
7. Uses a pastry blender to blend flour and shortening together.
8. Uses a glass to cut circles into the dough.
9. Uses spatula to turn pancakes over.
10. Stirs ingredients.

Teaching Suggestions

- Ask students what they like for breakfast.
- Discuss the importance of eating a nutritious breakfast.
- Choose foods from all four foods groups: meat (scrambled eggs) and bread and cereal (pancakes or biscuits) can be supplemented by milk and fresh fruit or juice.

Introduces the concept of preparing a complete and nutritious breakfast. Emphasizes the importance of eating a good breakfast.

Recipe Narrative

This eggs and pancakes recipe is a breakfast classic and encourages cooks to choose foods for all four groups.

Lesson 35

Seasonal

Recipe:
Garden Salad

or Mixed Fruit

Primary Objectives

1. Selects fruits and vegetables in season and knows they are best at certain times of the year.
2. Varies fruits and vegetables selected for salads according to the seasonal availability and cost.

Secondary Objectives

1. Washes fruits and vegetables before using them.
2. Uses a knife, fork and cutting board to slice fruits and vegetables.
3. Peels fruits and vegetables by hand.
4. Tears lettuce into pieces.
5. Shakes bottled dressing before pouring.

Teaching Suggestions

- Ask the students which fruits are available in winter. Are oranges? Grapes? Bananas? Apples? How about summer? Strawberries, blueberries, peaches, plums, nectarines, watermelon, cantaloupe.

- Make salads with the class that take advantage of fruits and vegetables in season.

- Ask the students which vegetables are available seasonally and which are available all year round.

- Put together different combinations of vegetables for a garden salad and orient users to color and texture.

- Discuss why fruits and vegetables, which are bought in season, usually taste better. They are cheaper, too.

76

Introduces the concept of buying seasonal foods, taking advantage of their freshness, taste and low cost.

☺ ☺ ☺ ☺
Serves 4

Garden Salad

1 head lettuce
celery
tomato
onion
dressing
cutting board
bowl
colander
¼ cup
knife

1. Wash the lettuce, tomato and celery
2. Tear lettuce to small pieces into the bowl
3. Peel and slice the onion

4. Slice the celery
5. Slice the tomato
6. Add the tomato, celery and onion to the lettuce

7. Shake the bottle of dressing
8. Pour 1 green cup dressing over the salad. Serve

3

Recipe Narrative

This recipe points out the tastiness of seasonal vegetables and emphasizes their use in salads.

Lesson 36

Serving Styles

Recipe:

Cranberry Sauce

Practice setting the table correctly.

Primary Objectives

1. Varies service styles (such as table settings, etc.), including: family style—places dishes in a central location to pass; buffet—places dishes on a separate table so people serve themselves; formal—arranges food on each plate in the kitchen and serves.
2. Knows that flowers, candles, different table linens and holiday decorations can make dining a more pleasurable or special experience.
3. Sets table correctly.

Secondary Objectives

1. Washes cranberries.
2. Measures ingredients accurately.
3. Operates color-coded stove.
4. Sets timer.
5. Stirs ingredients.
6. Uses oven mitts.

Teaching Suggestions

● Practice setting a table correctly. Instruct students to set the table for all the above listed occasions: family, buffet, formal.

● Discuss parties or holiday celebrations students have attended. What was served, and how? Was it family style? Buffet? Or formal? What was on the table besides food? Were there flowers? Candles? Holiday decorations?

● Show users pictures of table settings in magazine advertisements and ask "What kind of occasion do they represent?"

● Ask students which holiday cranberry sauce reminds them of.

78

Introduces the concept that serving styles must vary to adjust to special occasions, holidays, the number of guests and the type of dinner planned, including formal and family affairs.

Cranberry Sauce

Serves 8

cranberries | sugar | pot | colander | bowl | wooden spoon | oven mitts | 1 cup | 1/2 cup

1. Put 3 red cups cranberries in the colander. Wash.

2. Put the cranberries into the pot.

3. Add 1 red cup and 1 yellow cup water. Add 1 red cup sugar.

4. Put the pot on the stove. Turn to **red**.

5. Set the timer for 10 minutes.

6. Stir.

7. When the bell rings, turn to **white**. OFF

8. Put on oven mitts. Pour the sauce into a bowl.

9. Refrigerate. Serve.

6

Recipe Narrative

This recipe is a holiday favorite and is frequently used as a side dish in conjunction with turkey, duck, goose or chicken.

Recipes:

Chili

Biscuits

Primary Objectives

1. Prepares a series of recipes simultaneously or in order from the one that takes the most to the one that takes the least amount of time.
2. Freezes chili in advance, on occasion, as a time saver.
3. Follows the Meal Plan.

Meal Plan

1. Prepare chili through step #13.
2. Prepare biscuit recipe to completion.
3. When the bell rings, finish the chili recipe.
4. Serve the meal.

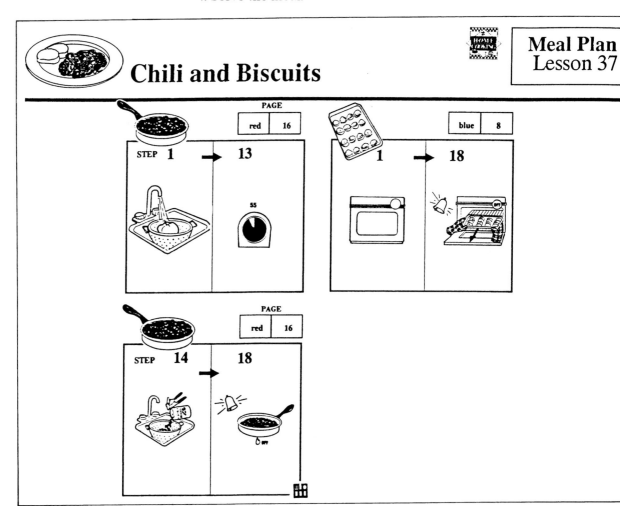

Chili and Biscuits

Meal Plan Lesson 37

Lesson 38

Making Meals

Primary Objectives

1. Prepares a series of recipes either simultaneously or in order from the one that takes the longest to the one that takes the least amount of time.
2. Decides which recipes should be prepared in advance because they need to be chilled.
3. Follows the recipe time line presented in the book.
4. Operates two timers—a hand-held one and the one on the stove or two hand-held ones.

Recipes:

Cranberry Sauce
_____

Ham
_____

Sweet Potatoes
_____

French Style Peas
_____

Meal Plan—Simultaneously

1. Prepare cranberry sauce in advance and refrigerate.
2. Begin sweet potato recipe and proceed to step #3.
3. Prepare the baked ham recipe to step #6.
4. Return to the sweet potatoes and do steps #4, 5 and 6 and set second timer.
5. When the bell rings, continue ham recipe steps #7-10 and reset the timer for twenty minutes (step 11).
6 When the bell rings, continue sweet potato recipe to completion.
7. When the bell rings, continue baked ham recipe to completion.
8. Prepare the french style peas recipe.
9. Serve the meal.

Meal Plan—In Order

1. Cranberry Sauce
2. Ham
3. Sweet Potatoes
4. French Style Peas

Note: This is the most challenging meal in the book and it is an ideal one to serve to company during the holidays. Roast cornish hen, a supplemental recipe, can be substituted for the ham and it works equally well.

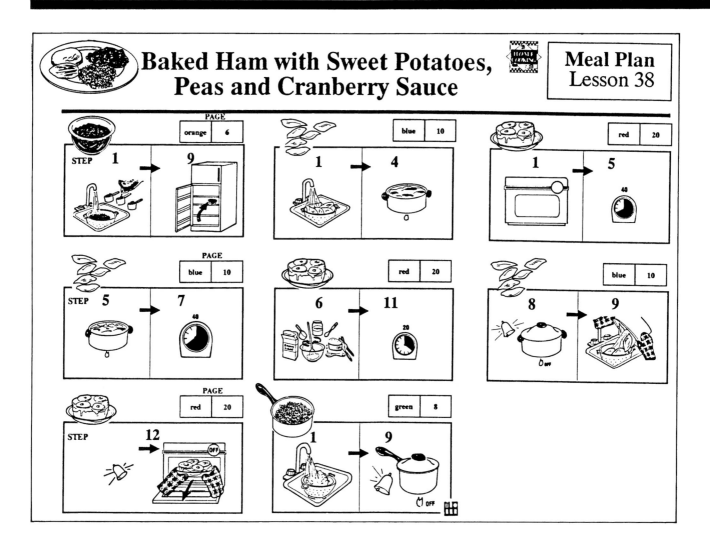

Baked Ham with Sweet Potatoes, Peas and Cranberry Sauce

Meal Plan
Lesson 38

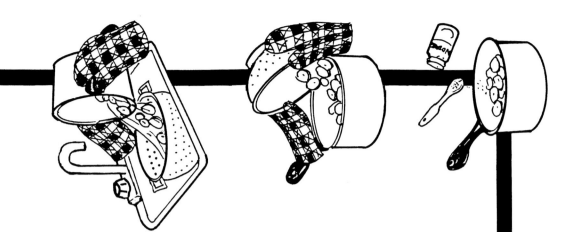

·H·O·M·E· COOKING

Resource File

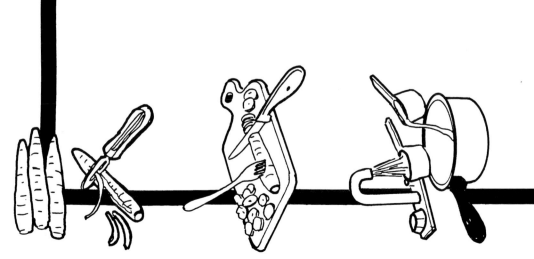

COOKING REPORT

Instructor _____

Class Period _____

Name	Date	Goal

Cooking Data Sheet Directions
The Data Sheet on the reverse side includes space to assess all aspects of a student's cooking performance. You may use all columns or select only the ones which are applicable.

Date and Name	Use one sheet per student or one sheet for each class.
Recipe	Title of recipe and page number in cookbook.
Lesson #	Number of lesson in the Instructor's Guide.
Recipe Steps	Each box represents a Home Cooking recipe step. Circle the box that corresponds to the last step of the chosen recipe to indicate the total number of steps in that recipe.
	Use Performance Scale code or simply check each box if a step is completed correctly.

PERFORMANCE SCALE

I	Independent performance
V	Verbal prompts needed
P	Physical prompts needed
U	Unable to complete
	Did not participate

Home Cooking Report - *page 2*

Date	Name	Recipe	Lesson #	Recipe Steps	Comments
				1 2 3 4 5 6 7 8 9 10 11 12 / 13 14 15 16 17 18 19 20 21 22 23 24	
				1 2 3 4 5 6 7 8 9 10 11 12 / 13 14 15 16 17 18 19 20 21 22 23 24	
				1 2 3 4 5 6 7 8 9 10 11 12 / 13 14 15 16 17 18 19 20 21 22 23 24	
				1 2 3 4 5 6 7 8 9 10 11 12 / 13 14 15 16 17 18 19 20 21 22 23 24	
				1 2 3 4 5 6 7 8 9 10 11 12 / 13 14 15 16 17 18 19 20 21 22 23 24	
				1 2 3 4 5 6 7 8 9 10 11 12 / 13 14 15 16 17 18 19 20 21 22 23 24	
				1 2 3 4 5 6 7 8 9 10 11 12 / 13 14 15 16 17 18 19 20 21 22 23 24	

Spaghetti with Meatballs in Sauce

blue	1

9 →

blue	2

16 →

30

+

PAGE	
red	1

STEP 1 → 13

PAGE	
blue	3

STEP 17 →

OFF

Chicken with Mashed Potatoes and Carrots

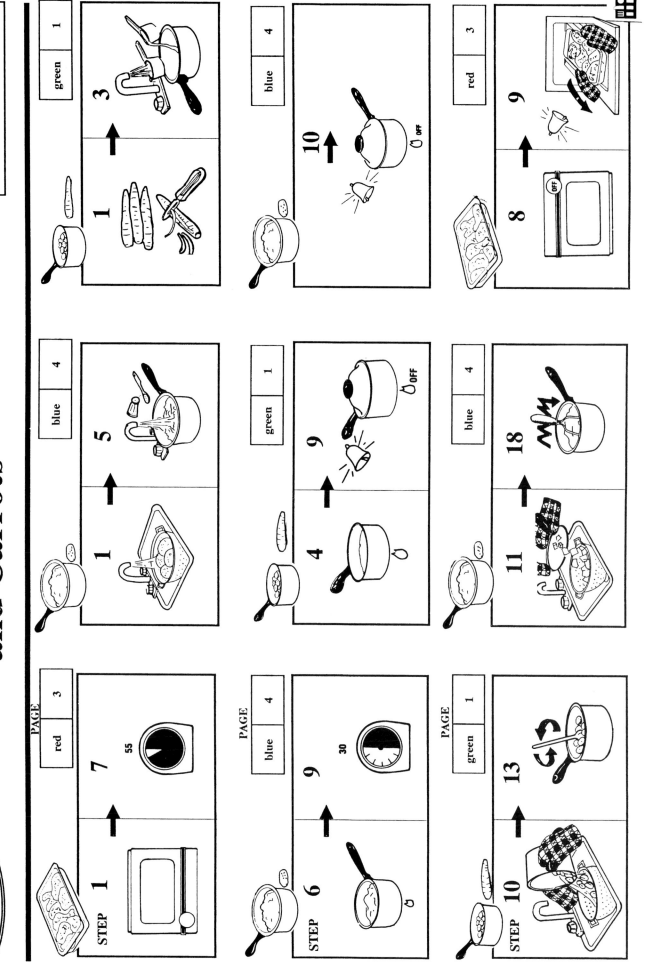

Hamburgers with Cole Slaw

PAGE	
orange	1

STEP 1 ↑ 9

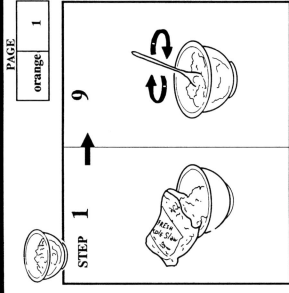

	red
	2

1 ↑ 12

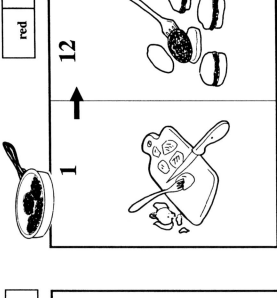

PAGE	
orange	6

STEP 9 ↑

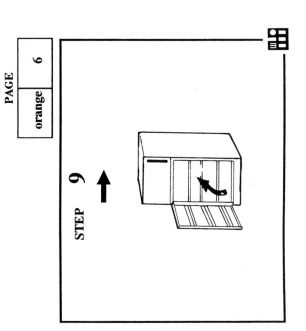

Orange Pork Chops with Rice and Green Beans

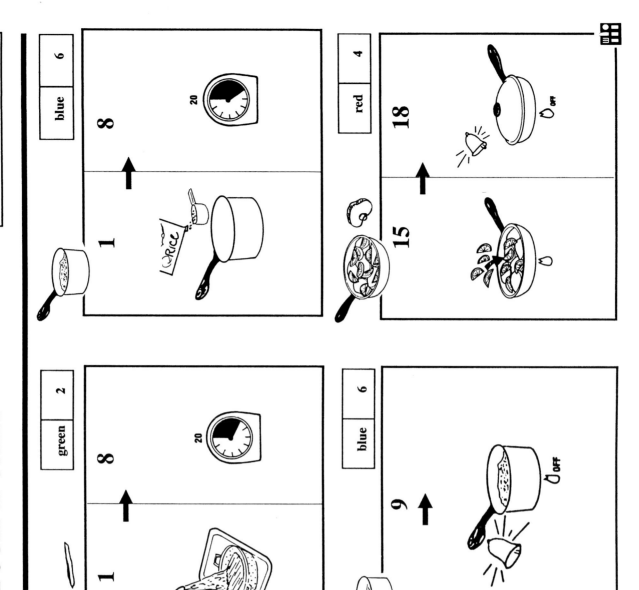

PAGE	4	red

STEP 1 14 · 45

1 · 8 · 20 | green | 2 |

1 · 8 · 20 | blue | 6 |

PAGE	2	green

STEP 9 13

9 · OFF · 9 | blue | 6 |

15 · 18 | red | 4 |

Fish Filets with Succotash

PAGE	
green	4

STEP 1   8 →

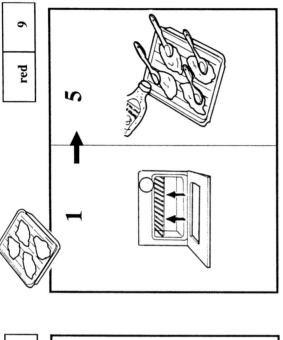

5

	red
	9

1 → 5

PAGE	
green	9

STEP 9 →

OFF

	red
	9

6 → 8

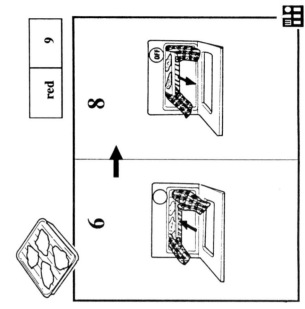

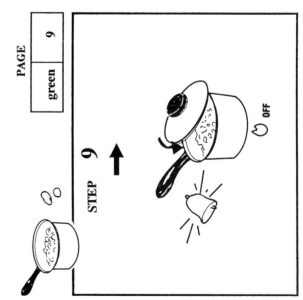

OFF

Tuna Salad Sandwich
with Corn on the Cob

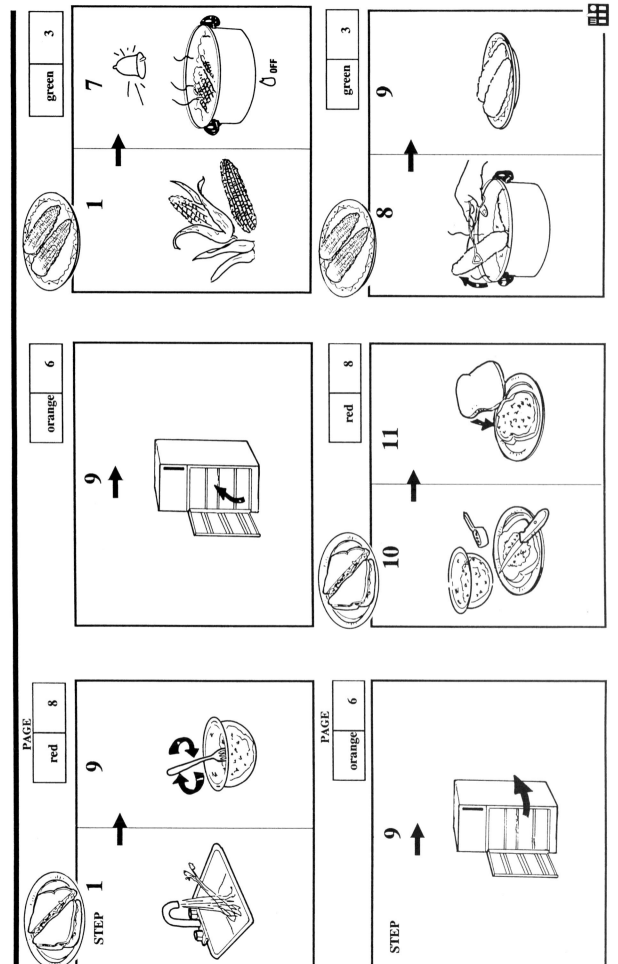

Meat Loaf with Baked Potato and Vegetable Platter

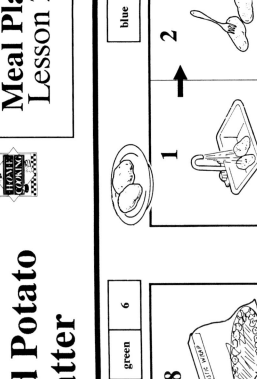

| blue | 7 |

1 2

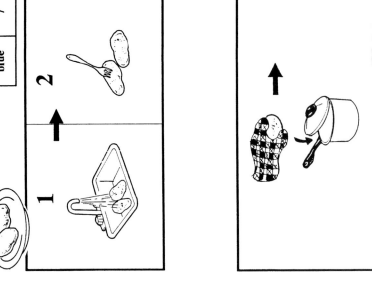

| green | 6 |

1 8

| blue | 7 |

3 9

| red | 15 |

18

| PAGE | 14 |
| red | |

STEP 1 15

| PAGE | 15 |
| red | |

STEP 16 17 5

| PAGE | 6 |
| green | |

STEP 9 14

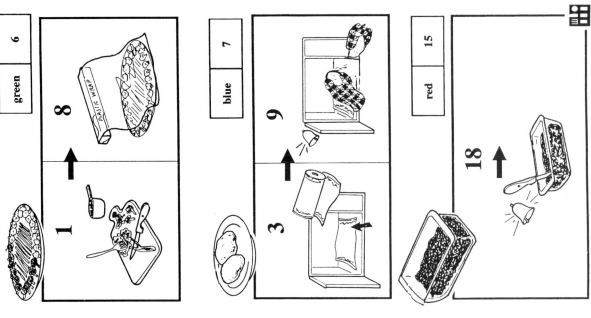

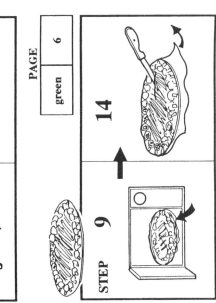

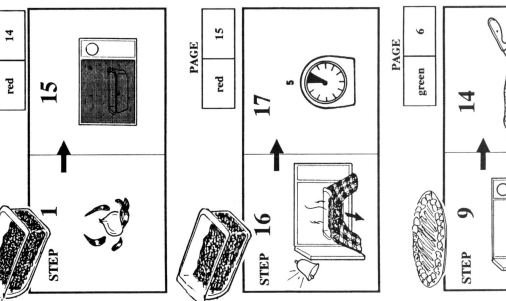

BBQ Chicken with Asparagus and Potato Salad

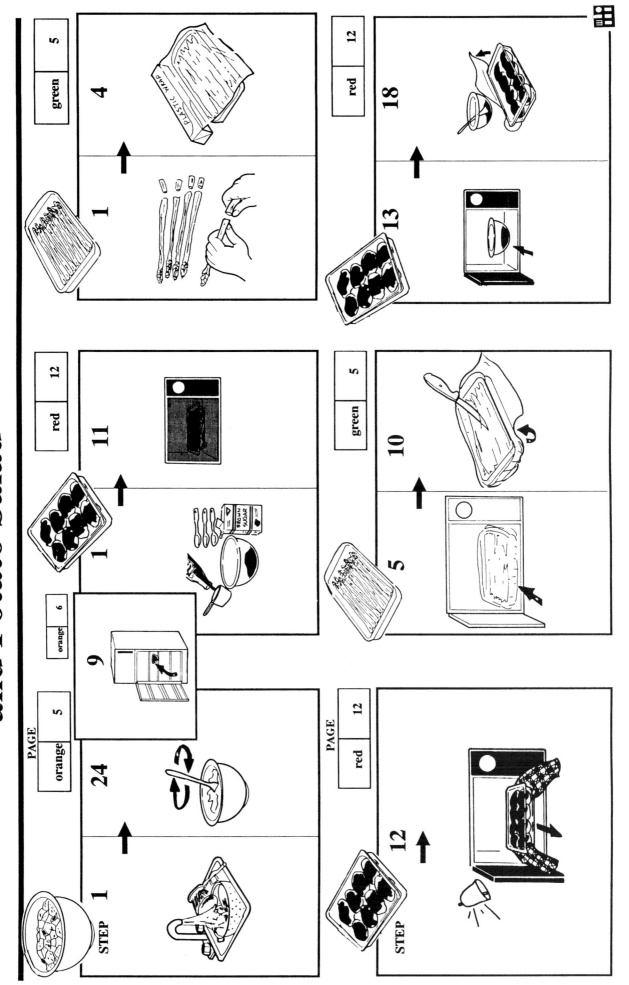

Chili and Biscuits

blue	8

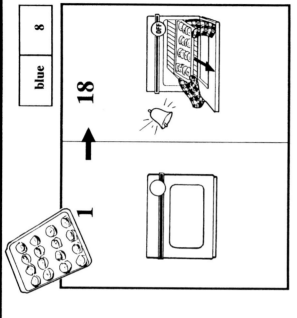

1 → 18

PAGE	
red	16

STEP 1 → 13

55

PAGE	
red	16

STEP 14 → 18

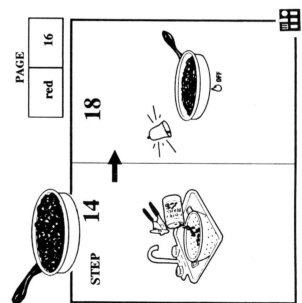

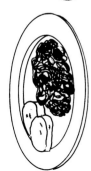

Baked Ham with Sweet Potatoes, Peas and Cranberry Sauce

Meal Plan
Lesson 38

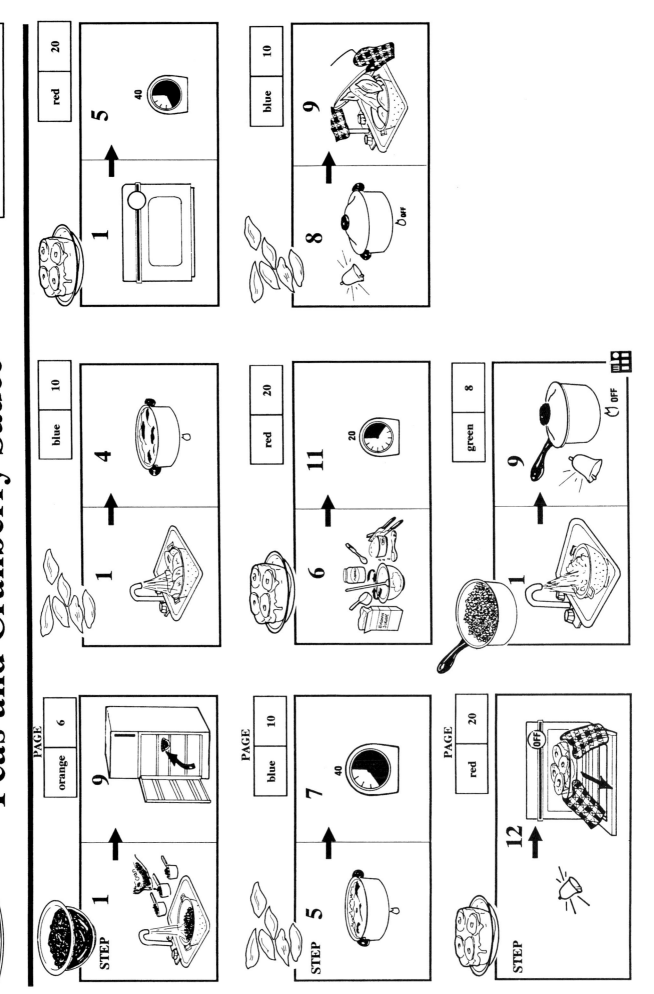

PICTURE COOKBOOK

Recipes
Ellen M. Sudol

To my father for his love and encouragement

Illustrations
Jo Reynolds

Published by Attainment Company, Inc., Verona, Wisconsin

Menu Maker

Main Dish	Side Dish	Vegetable	Salad	Dessert
1 Meatballs	**1 - 3** Spaghetti			
2 Hamburgers			**1** Cole Slaw	**1** Impossible Pie
3 Herb Chicken	**4 - 5** Mashed Potatoes	**1** Carrots with Nutmeg		**2 - 3** Chocolate Chip Cookies
4 - 5 Orange Pork Chops	**6** Rice	**2** Green Beans	**2** Spinach Salad	
6 - 7 Roast Beef			**3** Garden Salad	**4 - 5** Apple Crumb Pie
8 Tuna Salad Sandwich		**3** Corn on the Cob		**6** Frozen Strawberry Drink

Menu Maker

Main Dish	Side Dish	Vegetable	Salad	Dessert
red	*blue*	*green*	*orange*	*pink*
9 Broiled Fish Filets		**4** Succotash		
10 - 11 Chicken Soup				
12 - 13 Barbecued Chicken		**5** Microwave Asparagus	**4 - 5** Potato Salad	
14 - 15 Microwave Meat Loaf	**7** Baked Potatoes	**6 - 7** Microwave Vegetable Platter		
16 - 17 Chili	**8 - 9** Biscuits			
18 - 19 Vegetable Soup				**7** Mixed Fruit
20 Baked Ham	**10** Sweet Potatoes	**8** French Style Peas	**6** Cranberry Sauce	**8** Pumpkin Pie

Using the Cookbook

Following a Recipe

The completed dish is shown at the top left of the page. Start your recipe by getting out the ingredients and cooking supplies shown in the top row. Follow the recipe steps across the page from left to right. Read across both pages if the recipe is two pages long. The page numbers are color coded, too, so they match the **Menu Maker**.

One Page Recipe

Complete dish

The steps read from left to right

Page number in the red section

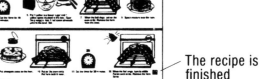

Number of people served

Supplies

The recipe is finished

Two Page Recipe

Microwave symbol

Completed dish

The steps read from left to right

Arrow moves across page for the next step

Page number in the green section

Number of people served

Supplies

The recipe is finished

Page number in the green section

Time

Timer   **Bell**

Your **timer** should be in five minutes intervals. Dial your timer to match the minutes shown above the timer picture.

The **bell** is a symbol for the ringing of your timer. Go to the next step when you hear the bell.

Set cooking time on the **microwave** by following the numbers on the recipe page.

Microwave

5
0
0

These numbers mean 5 minutes.

Color-Your-Own

Color recipe measurements with red, blue, yellow or green markers to match the equipment coding on the opposite page. Color temperatures to match the color indicated in the text below stove or microwave illustrations.

Other ingredients may be colored as you choose to help identify food or utensils used in a recipe.

You may also photocopy recipe pages so everyone can have their own copy to color and use. Then, each step can be crossed off as it is completed.

Make your equipment match our colors.

Color Coding

Temperatures

Measurements

Stove Top

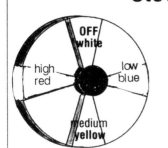

 **High - red**

 Medium - yellow

Low - blue

OFF - white

Put colored plastic tape on the stove dial according to the above chart. Match the color of the flame in the recipe to the color on the dial.

Oven

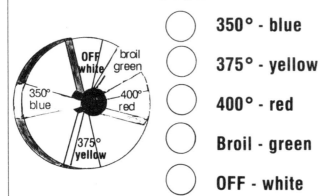

○ **350° - blue**

○ **375° - yellow**

○ **400° - red**

○ **Broil - green**

○ **OFF - white**

Put colored tape on the oven dial also. Match the color on the picture of the stove to the color on your stove dial.

Microwave

Yellow	Blue	Green
○	○	○
Clear	Time	Start

Put color tape on these microwave buttons or your microwave dial.

 **1 cup - red**

 **1/2 cup - yellow**

1/3 cup - blue

1/4 cup - green

 **Tablespoon - red**

1 teaspoon - yellow

1/2 teaspoon - blue

 **1/4 teaspoon - green**

All of the measurements in this book are color coded. Match the color on the spoon or cup to the color shown in the recipe.

Use Colored Tape

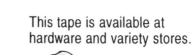

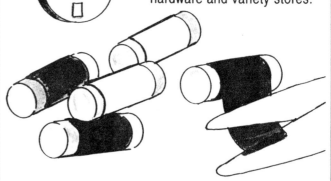

Match our color coding by putting red, yellow, blue, green, and white plastic tape on your own equipment.

This tape is available at hardware and variety stores.

Setting the Table

Place Setting

Other Options for the Table

sweetner packets

non-dairy creamer

milk

butter

salt

pepper

ketchup
catsup

mustard

bread

hot sauce

napkin holder

sugar

cream

beverage

water

salad dressing

Serves 4

Meatballs

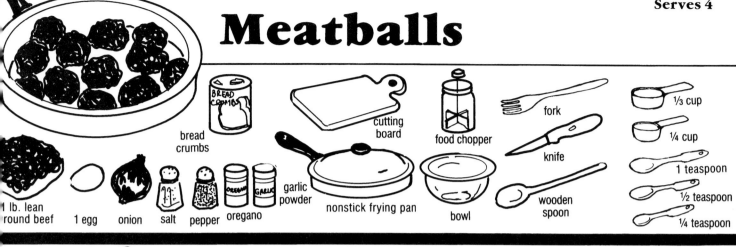

bread crumbs · cutting board · food chopper · fork · knife · wooden spoon · 1/3 cup · 1/4 cup · 1 teaspoon · 1/2 teaspoon · 1/4 teaspoon · 1 lb. lean ground beef · 1 egg · onion · salt · pepper · oregano · garlic powder · nonstick frying pan · bowl

1. Peel the onion. Cut into pieces. Chop pieces in the food chopper.

2. Put the chopped onion and ground beef in the bowl. Add 1 blue cup bread crumbs.

3. Add 1 egg, 1 blue spoon salt and 1 green spoon pepper.

4. Add 1 yellow spoon oregano and 1 blue spoon garlic powder.

5. Mix.

6. Use the green cup to measure the meat. Roll into balls.

7. Put the frying pan on the stove. Turn to **yellow**.

8. Put the meatballs into the pan.

9. Set the timer for 5 minutes.

10. When the bell rings, use the wooden spoon to turn the meatballs.

11. Cover. Turn to **blue**.

12. Set the timer for 15 minutes.

13. When the bell rings, turn to **white**. Serve. (Or add to spaghetti sauce.)

Serves 4

Hamburgers

4 buns | egg | onion | 1 lb. ground beef | salt | pepper | food chopper | bowl | cutting board | nonstick frying pan | spatula | fork | knife | Tablespoon | ¼ teaspoon

1. Peel the onion. Cut the onion into pieces.

2. Put onion pieces into the food chopper. Chop the onion.

3. Put 3 red spoons onion in the bowl. Add 1 lb. ground beef.

4. Add the egg, 1 green spoon salt and 1 green spoon pepper.

5. Mix.

6. Shape into 4 hamburgers.

7. Put the pan on the stove. Turn to **yellow**. Place the hamburgers in the pan.

8. Set the timer for 5 minutes.

9. When the bell rings, turn the hamburgers.

10. Set the timer for 5 minutes.

11. When the bell rings, turn to **white**.

12. Place hamburgers on the buns. Serve.

2 red

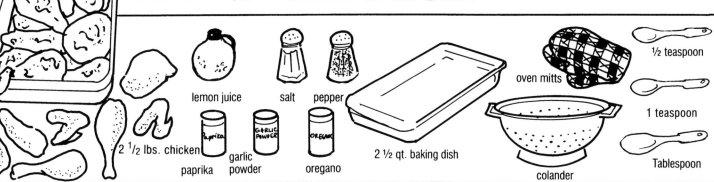

Herb Chicken

Serves 4

2 ½ lbs. chicken
lemon juice
salt
pepper
paprika
garlic powder
oregano
2 ½ qt. baking dish
oven mitts
colander
½ teaspoon
1 teaspoon
Tablespoon

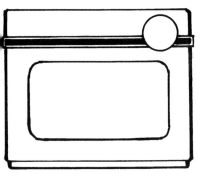

1. Preheat the oven. Turn to **yellow**.

2. Wash the chicken.

3. Arrange the chicken in a 2 ½ qt. baking dish.

4. Sprinkle with 3 red spoons lemon juice, 1 blue spoon garlic powder and 1 yellow spoon paprika.

5. Sprinkle with 1 yellow spoon oregano, 1 blue spoon salt and 1 blue spoon pepper.

6. Put on the oven mitts. Place the chicken in the oven.

55

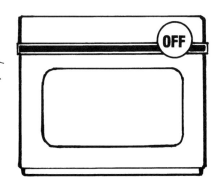

7. Set the timer for 55 minutes.

8. When the bell rings, turn the oven to **white**.

9. Put on the oven mitts. Remove the chicken from the oven. Serve.

red

3

Orange Pork Chops

2 oranges   olive oil   6 pork chops   brown sugar   ginger   allspice

6 oz. can frozen orange juice, tha

1. Peel the 2 oranges, then slice.

2. Cut orange slices in half.

3. Put the frying pan on the stove. Turn to **yellow**.

7. When the bell rings, turn the pork chops.

8. Put the thawed orange juice and 2 red spoons brown sugar into the bowl.

9. Put 1 yellow spoon ginger and 1 blue spoon allspice into the bowl.

13. Put the lid on the frying pan.

45

14. Set the timer for 45 minutes.

15. When the bell rings, put the orange slices on the pork chops.

bowl

cutting board

nonstick frying pan with lid

wooden spoon

spatula

knife

¹/₂ teaspoon

1 teaspoon

Tablespoon

4. Put 1 red spoon olive oil into the frying pan.

5. Put the 6 pork chops in the frying pan.

6. Set the timer for 5 minutes.

10. Stir.

11. Pour the mixture into the frying pan.

12. Turn to **blue.**

16. Put the lid on the frying pan.

17. Set the timer for 5 minutes.

18. When the bell rings, turn to **white.** Serve.

red

5

Roast Beef

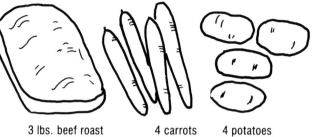   

onion   3 lbs. beef roast   4 carrots   4 potatoes   salt   pepper   oven mitts

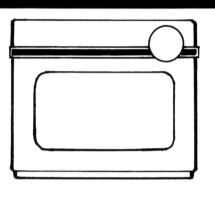

1. Preheat the oven. Turn to **blue**.

2. Peel and rinse the carrots.

3. Cut each carrot into 4 pieces.

7. Sprinkle the beef with 1 blue spoon salt and 1 green spoon pepper.

8. Put the carrots and potatoes in the broiler pan.

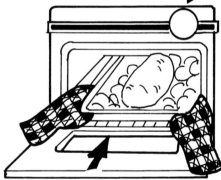

9. Put on oven mitts. Put the pan in the oven.

13. Turn the potatoes and carrots.

14. Add the onion to the pan.

15. Return the pan to the oven.

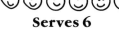

Serves 6

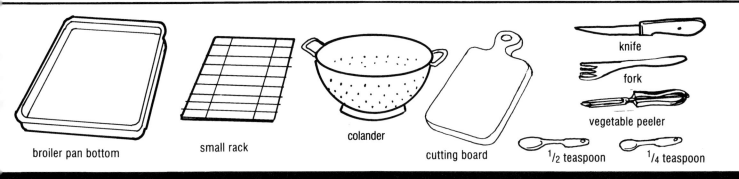

broiler pan bottom   small rack   colander   cutting board   ¹/₂ teaspoon   ¹/₄ teaspoon

knife
fork
vegetable peeler

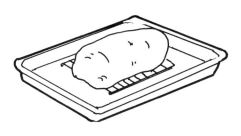

4. Peel the potatoes.

5. Cut each potato into 4 pieces.

6. Put the beef on a small rack in the broiler pan.

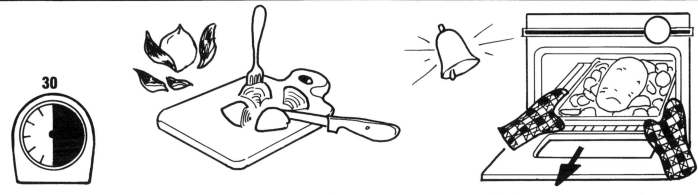

0. Set the timer for 30 minutes.

11. Peel the onion. Cut it into 4 pieces.

12. When the bell rings, put on the oven mitts. Remove the pan.

16. Set the timer for 40 minutes.

17. When the bell rings, turn to **white**. Put on the oven mitts. Remove the pan.

18. Slice the beef. Serve.

Tuna Salad Sandwich

Serves

pepper

tuna

mayonnaise

celery stalk

onion
fork
knife
can opener

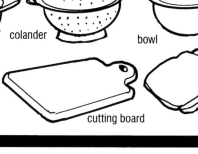
colander
cutting board

bowl
bread

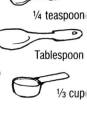
¼ teaspoon
Tablespoon
⅓ cup

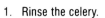

1. Rinse the celery.

2. Cut the celery into small pieces.

3. Peel the onion.

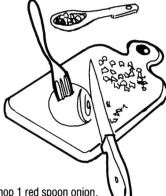

4. Chop 1 red spoon onion.

5. Open the tuna. Pour it into the colander and drain.

6. Pour the tuna into the bowl. Break the tuna into small pieces.

7. Add the celery and red spoon onion.

8. Add 1 blue cup lite mayonnaise and 1 green spoon pepper.

9. Stir.

10. Spread 1 blue cup tuna on a slice of bread.

11. Put another piece of bread on top to make a sandwich. Serve.

8

Broiled Fish Filets

4 fish filets   Italian dressing   broiler pan   oven mitts   spatula   ¹/₄ teaspoon

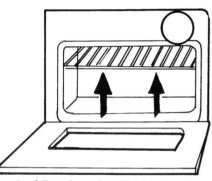

1. Adjust the rack to high level. Preheat the broiler. Turn to **green**.

2. Put the fish filets on the broiler pan.

3. Spread 1 green spoon Italian dressing on each filet.

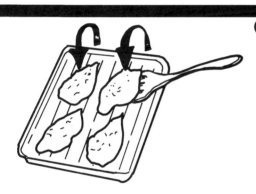

4. Turn over the filets.

5. Spread 1 green spoon Italian dressing on each filet.

6. Put on the oven mitts. Put the filets on the rack.

6. Set the timer for 5 minutes.

7. When the bell rings, turn to **white**.

8. Put on oven mitts. Remove fish filets. Serve.

red   **9**

Chicken Soup

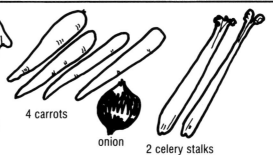

2 lbs. chicken pieces

4 carrots

onion

2 celery stalks

chicken bouillon

pepper   salt

1. Rinse the chicken.

2. Put the chicken into the pot.

3. Rinse the carrots and celery.

7. Put the carrots, celery and onions into the pot.

8. Add 4 red cups water.

9. Add 1 yellow spoon salt and 1 green spoon pepper.

13. When the soup begins to boil . . .

14. Put the lid on the pot. Turn to **blue**.

55

15. Set the timer for 55 minutes.

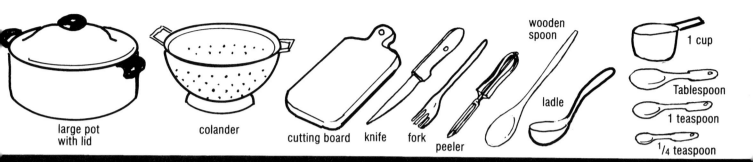

Serves 8

large pot
with lid

colander

cutting board   knife   fork

peeler

wooden
spoon

ladle

1 cup

Tablespoon

1 teaspoon

1/4 teaspoon

4. Peel and slice the carrots.

5. Slice the celery.

6. Peel and slice the onion.

10. Add 1 red spoon chicken bouillon.

11. Stir.

12. Put the pot on the stove. Turn to **red**.

OFF

16. When the bell rings, turn to **white**.

17. Serve.

red | **11**

Barbecued Chicken

garlic powder

8 chicken thighs

salt   pepper

ketchup

brown sugar

vinegar

oven mitts

1. Put 1 red cup ketchup in the bowl. Add 3 red spoons brown sugar.

2. Add 2 red spoons vinegar and 1 blue spoon garlic powder.

3. Add 1 blue spoon salt and 1 green spoon pepper. Stir.

7. Cover the dish tightly with plastic wrap.

8. Put the chicken in the microwave. Push **yellow**.

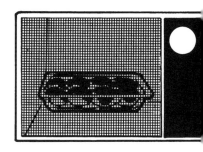

9. Push **blue**.

13. Put the sauce in the microwave. Push **yellow**.

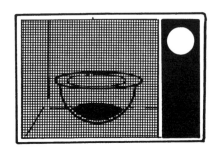

14. Push **blue**.

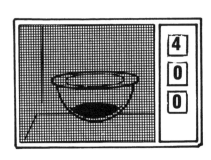

15. Push **4 0 0**.

colander

glass bowl

wooden spoon

2 ¹/₂ qt. baking dish

plastic wrap

Plastic Wrap

1 cup

¹/₂ cup

Tablespoon

¹/₂ teaspoon

¹/₄ teaspoon

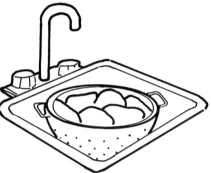

4. Rinse the chicken.

5. Put the chicken in the baking dish.

6. Spread 1 yellow cup sauce over the chicken.

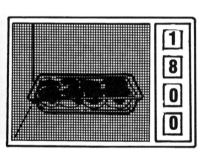

10. Push **1 8 0 0**.

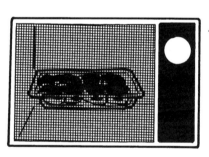

11. Push **green**.

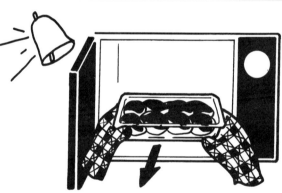

12. When the bell rings put on the oven mitts. Remove the chicken.

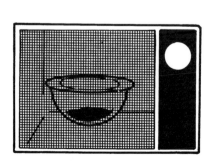

16. Push **green.**

17. When the bell rings, put on the oven mitts. Remove the sauce.

18. Serve the chicken with sauce on the side.

Microwave Meat Loaf

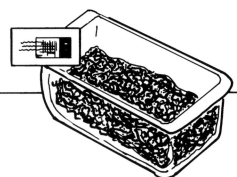

1 lb. lean ground beef

egg

milk

bread crumbs

salt   pepper

onion

ketchup

bowl

cutting board

1. Peel the onion.

2. Cut off a piece of onion.

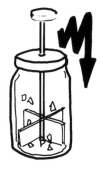

3. Chop the onion piece in the food chopper.

7. Add 2 red spoons ketchup.

8. Mix.

9. Put the mixture into a glass loaf pan.

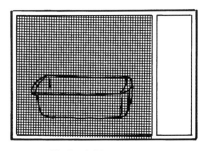

13. Push **blue**.

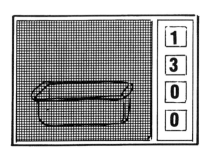

14. Push **1 3 0 0**.

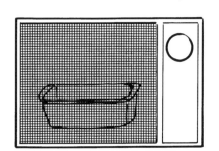

15. Push **green**.

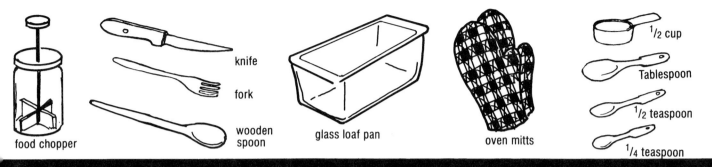

food chopper | knife | fork | wooden spoon | glass loaf pan | oven mitts | ¹/₂ cup | Tablespoon | ¹/₂ teaspoon | ¹/₄ teaspoon

Put 1 red spoon onion in the bowl.
Add 1 lb. lean ground beef.

5. Put 2 red spoons milk into the bowl.
Add 1 yellow cup bread crumbs.

6. Add 1 egg, 1 blue spoon salt
and 1 green spoon pepper.

10. Pat down.

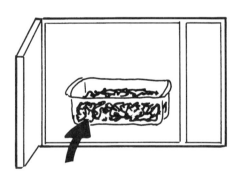

11. Put the loaf pan in the microwave.

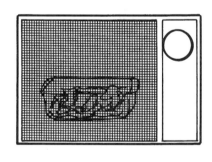

12. Close the door. Push **yellow**.

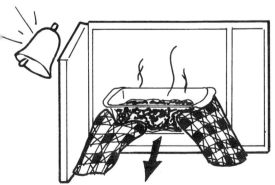

16. When the bell rings, put on oven
mitts. Remove the meat loaf.

17. Set the timer for 5 minutes.

18. When the bell rings, slice the
meat loaf. Serve.

Chili

1 lb. ground round

green pepper

onion

16 oz. can tomatoes

15 oz. can kidney beans

salt

pepper

chili powder

cumin

garlic powder

1. Rinse the green pepper.

2. Chop the green pepper.

3. Peel and chop the onion.

10

7. Set the timer for 10 minutes.

8. When the bell rings, open and add the can of tomatoes and 1 blue spoon garlic powder.

9. Add 2 red spoons chili powder and 1 yellow spoon cumin.

55

13. Set the timer for 55 minutes.

14. Open and drain the kidney beans.

15. When the bell rings, add the kidney beans.

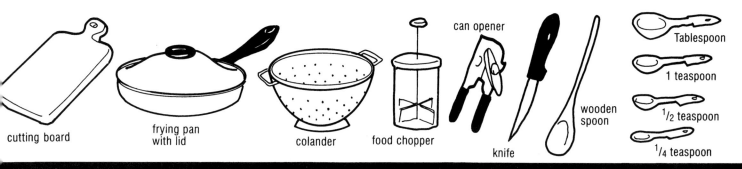

cutting board

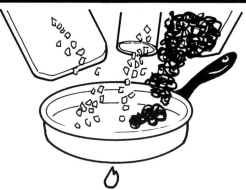

frying pan
with lid

colander

food chopper

can opener

knife

wooden
spoon

Tablespoon

1 teaspoon

1/2 teaspoon

1/4 teaspoon

4. Put the frying pan on the stove.
   Turn to **yellow.**

5. Put the green pepper and onion into the pan.
   Add the ground round.

6. Stir.

10. Add 1 green spoon pepper and
    and 1 yellow spoon salt.

11. Stir.

12. Put the lid on the pan.
    Turn to **blue**.

16. Stir.

17. Set the timer for 15 minutes.

OFF

Vegetable Soup

onion
2 carrots
2 small zucchinis
2 celery stalks
1/2 lb. green beans
olive oil
two 17 oz. cans tomatoes
two 16 oz. cans chicken broth
parsley   pepper
basil   oregano   garlic powder

1. Wash the carrots, celery, green beans and zucchini.

2. Peel the carrots. Chop the carrots.

3. Chop the celery.

7. Add the carrots, celery and onion. Stir.

8. Set the timer for 5 minutes.

9. When the bell rings, open and add 2 cans tomatoes and 1 green spoon pepper.

13. When the bell rings, open and add 2 cans chicken broth. Add the green beans.

14. Set the timer for 30 minutes.

15. Slice the zucchini.

large pot   cutting board   colander   food chopper   fork   can opener   ladle   wooden spoon   knife   vegetable peeler   Tablespoon   1 teaspoon   ¼ teaspoon

4. Peel the onion. Chop the onion.

5. Put the large pot on the stove. Turn to **yellow**.

6. Put 2 red spoons olive oil into the pot.

10. Add 1 yellow spoon basil, 1 yellow spoon oregano and 1 yellow spoon garlic powder. Stir.

11. Set the timer for 15 minutes.

12. Cut off the ends of the green beans. Cut the beans into 4 pieces.

16. When the bell rings, add the zucchini and 1 red spoon parsley.

17. Stir.

18. Turn to **white**. Serve.

Baked Ham

3 lb. canned ham

pineapple slices

brown sugar

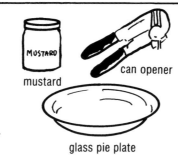
mustard   can opener

glass pie plate

bowl

wooden spoon   oven mitts

1/2 cup

Tablespoon

1 teaspoon

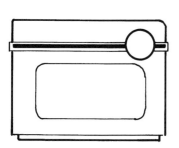

1. Preheat the oven. Turn to **blue.**

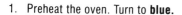

2. Open the canned ham.

3. Put the ham in the pie plate.

4. Put on oven mitts.
Put the ham in the oven.

40

5. Set the timer for 40 minutes.

6. Put 1 yellow cup brown sugar and 1 yellow spoon mustard in the bowl. Open the pineapple. Add 1 red spoon pineapple juice to the bowl. Stir.

7. When the bell rings, put on the oven mitts. Remove the ham from the oven.

8. Spoon mixture over the ham.

9. Put pineapple slices on the ham.

10. Put on the oven mitts.
Put ham back in oven.

20

11. Set the timer for 20 minutes.

12. When the bell rings, turn to **white.**
Put on oven mitts. Remove the ham.
Serve.

Spaghetti

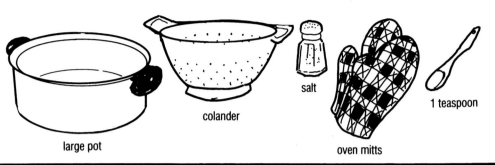

salt

colander

1 teaspoon

1 lb.
spaghetti

large pot

oven mitts

1. Fill the pot halfway with water.

2. Add 1 yellow spoon salt.

3. Put the pot on the stove. Turn to **red**.

4. When the water boils...

5. Add the spaghetti.

10

6. Set the timer for 10 minutes.

OFF

7. When the bell rings, turn the stove to
white.

8. Put on the oven mitts. Pour the
spaghetti into the colander.

9. Rinse with hot water. Drain. Serve
with sauce.

Spaghetti Sauce

two 6 oz. cans
tomato paste

parsley

onion

two 28 oz. cans tomatoes

olive oil

garlic
powder

oregano

basil

pepper

salt

1. Peel the onion. Cut into pieces. Chop the
   pieces in the food chopper.

2. Cut 1 green cup parsley.

3. Put the pot on the stove.
   Turn to **yellow.**

7. Stir.

5

8. Set the timer for 5 minutes.

9. When the bell rings, open the tomatoes.
   Add to the pot.

13. Add 1 blue spoon salt. Add 1 green
    spoon pepper.

14. Stir.

15. Turn to **blue.**

2 | blue

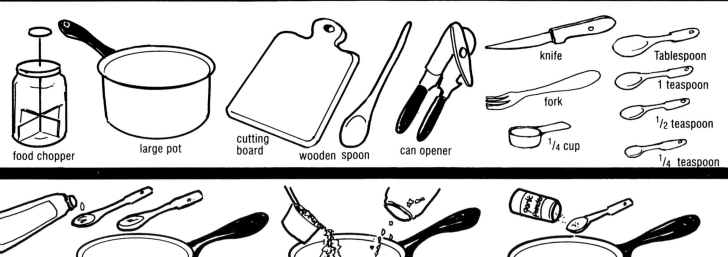

food chopper   large pot   cutting board   wooden spoon   can opener   knife   fork   ¼ cup   Tablespoon   1 teaspoon   ½ teaspoon   ¼ teaspoon

4. Put 2 red spoons olive oil into the pot.

5. Add the onion and parsley.

6. Add 1 yellow spoon garlic powder.

10. Open the tomato paste. Add to the pot.

11. Stir.

12. Add 2 red spoons oregano. Add 1 red spoon basil.

16. Set the timer for 30 minutes.

17. When the bell rings, turn to **white**. Serve.

Mashed Potatoes

4 potatoes   skim milk   salt   pepper   margarine   colander   oven mitts

1. Rinse the potatoes.

2. Peel the potatoes.

3. Cut the potatoes into pieces.

7. When the water begins to boil...

8. Put the lid on the pot. Turn to **blue**.

9. Set the timer for 30 minutes.

13. Mash the potatoes.

14. Add 1 yellow cup skim milk, 1 yellow spoon margarine, and 1 green spoon pepper.

15. Put the pot on the stove. Turn to **yellow**.

pot with lid   cutting board   knife   vegetable peeler   fork   potato masher   ½ cup   1 teaspoon   ¼ teaspoon

4. Put the potatoes into the pot.

5. Add water to cover the potatoes. Add 1 yellow spoon salt.

6. Put the pot on the stove. Turn to **red**.

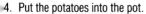

10. When the bell rings, turn to **white**. **OFF**

11. Put on oven mitts. Drain the potatoes in the colander.

12. Pour the potatoes back into the pot.

16. Set the timer for 1 minute.

17. When the bell rings, turn to **white**. **OFF**

18. Mash the potatoes. Serve.

Rice

rice

salt

butter

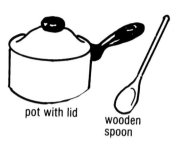
pot with lid

wooden spoon

1 cup

Tablespoon

1/2 teaspoon

1. Put 1 red cup rice in the pot.

2. Put 2 red cups water in the pot.

3. Put 1 red spoon butter in the pot

4. Add 1 blue spoon salt. Stir.

5. Put the pot on the stove. Turn to **red**.

6. When the water boils . . .

7. Put the lid on the pot. Turn to **blue.**

20

8. Set the timer for 20 minutes.

OFF

9. When the bell rings, turn to **white**. Serve.

Serves 2

Baked Potatoes

2 potatoes

fork

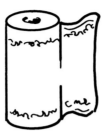

paper towel

oven mitts

plate

1. Wash the potatoes.

2. Prick the potatoes with a fork.

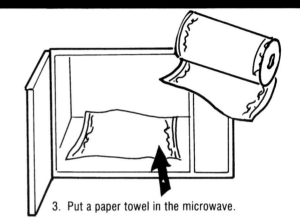

3. Put a paper towel in the microwave.

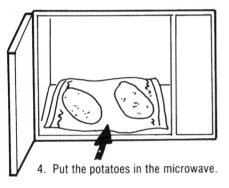

4. Put the potatoes in the microwave.

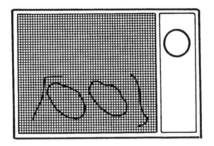

5. Close the door. Push **yellow**.

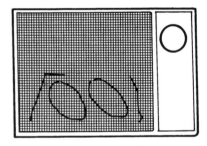

6. Push **blue.**

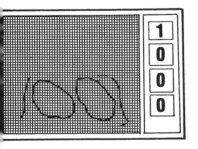

7. Push **1 0 0 0.**

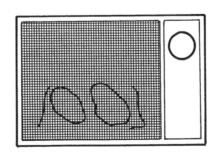

8. Push **green.**

9. When the bell rings, put on the oven mitts. Remove the potatoes. Serve.

blue

7

Biscuits

salt

baking powder

shortening

flour

milk

bowl

pastry blender

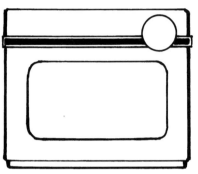

1. Preheat the oven. Turn to **red**.

2. Put 2 red cups flour in the bowl.

3. Add 1 red spoon baking powder.

7. Add 1 yellow cup and 1 green cup milk.

8. Stir.

9. Sprinkle 1 green cup flour on the table.

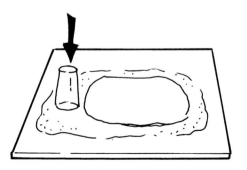

13. Dip the glass into flour.

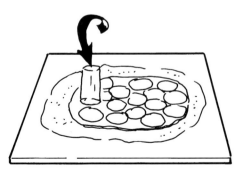

14. Use the glass to cut circles into the dough.

15. Put the biscuits on the baking sheet.

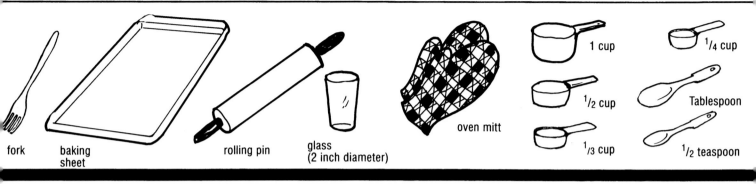

fork   baking sheet   rolling pin   glass (2 inch diameter)   oven mitt   1 cup   1/4 cup   1/2 cup   Tablespoon   1/3 cup   1/2 teaspoon

4. Add 1 blue spoon salt.

5. Add 1 blue cup shortening.

6. Blend the shortening and flour.

10. Put the dough on the flour.

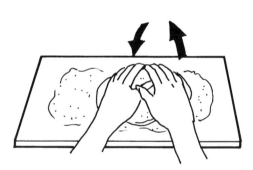

11. Knead the dough. (10 times)

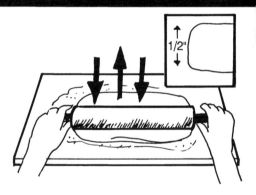

12. Roll out the dough. (1/2 inch thick).

16. Put on oven mitts. Put the biscuits in the oven.

17. Set the timer for 10 minutes.

18. When the bell rings, put on oven mitts. Remove the biscuits. Serve.

Sweet Potatoes

salt

6 sweet potatoes

large pot with lid

colander

1 teaspoon

oven mitts

1. Wash the sweet potatoes.

2. Put the sweet potatoes in a large pot.

3. Cover the sweet potatoes with water. Add 1 yellow spoon salt.

4. Put the pan on the stove. Turn to **red**.

5. When the water boils . . .

6. Put the lid on the pot. Turn to **blue**.

7. Set the timer for 40 minutes.

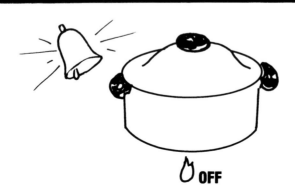

OFF

8. When the bell rings, turn to **white**.

9. Drain the potatoes. Serve.

Carrots with Nutmeg

Serves 4

nutmeg

4 carrots

colander

pot with lid

wooden spoon

oven mitts

knife

fork

cutting board

1 cup

¼ teaspoon

vegetable peeler

1. Peel four carrots.

2. Use knife and fork to slice the carrots.

3. Put 2 red cups water into the pot.

4. Put the pot on the stove. Turn to **red**.

5. When the water boils . . .

6. Put the carrots into the pot.

7. Put the lid on the pot. Turn to **blue**.

8. Set the timer for **20** minutes.

9. When the bell rings, turn to **white**.

10. Put on the oven mitts. Drain the carrots in the colander.

11. Pour the carrots back into the pot.

12. Add 1 green spoon nutmeg.

13. Stir and serve.

green

1

Green Beans

1 lb. green beans

pot with lid

Italian dressing

colander

cutting board

oven mitts

wooden spoon

knife

1 cup

Tablespo

1. Rinse the green beans.

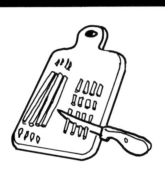

2. Cut the ends off the green beans. Then cut each green bean into 4 pieces.

3. Put 2 red cups water into the pot.

4. Put the pot on the stove. Turn to **red**.

5. Put the green beans into the pot.

6. When the water boils . . . .

7. Put the lid on the pot. Turn to **blue**.

8. Set the timer for 20 minutes.

9. When the bell rings, turn to **white**.

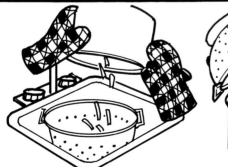

10. Put on oven mitts. Drain the green beans.

11. Pour the green beans back into the pot.

12. Add 2 red spoons Italian dressing.

13. Stir and serve.

Corn on the Cob

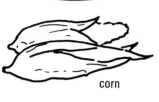
corn

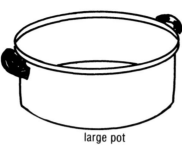
large pot

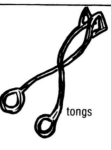
tongs

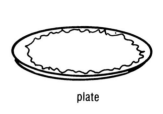
plate

1. Husk the corn (if necessary).

2. Fill the pot halfway with water.

3. Put the pot on the stove. Turn to **red**.

4. When the water boils…

5. Use the tongs to place the corn in the pot.

5

6. Set the timer for 5 minutes.

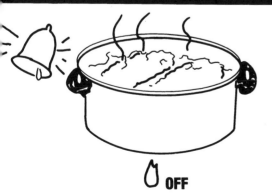
7. When the bell rings, turn to **white**.

8. Use the tongs to remove the corn.

9. Serve.

Succotash

10 oz. frozen lima beans

10 oz. frozen corn

pot with lid

wooden spoon

½ cup

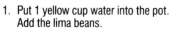

1. Put 1 yellow cup water into the pot. Add the lima beans.

2. Put the pot on the stove. Turn to **red**.

3. When the water boils...

4. Put the lid on the pot. Turn to **yellow**.

5

5. Set the timer for 5 minutes.

6. When the bell rings, add the corn. Stir.

7. Put the lid on the pot.

5

8. Set the timer for 5 minutes.

OFF

9. When the bell rings, turn to **white**. Serve.

Microwave Asparagus

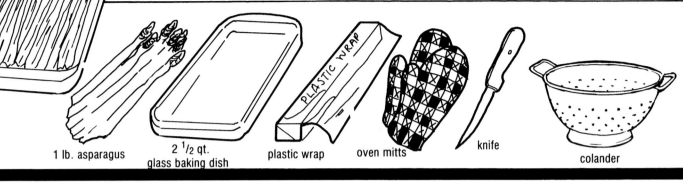

1 lb. asparagus   2 ½ qt. glass baking dish   plastic wrap   oven mitts   knife   colander

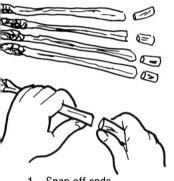

1. Snap off ends.

2. Wash the asparagus.

3. Lay the asparagus in the glass dish.

4. Cover the dish with the plastic wrap.

5. Put the dish in the microwave. Push **yellow**.

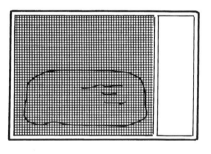

6. Push **blue**.

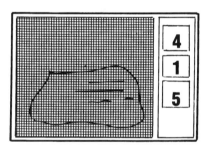

7. Push **4 1 5**.

8. Push **green**.

9. When the bell rings, put on oven mitts. Remove the dish.

10. Cut the plastic. Then remove the plastic. Serve.

Microwave Vegetable Platter

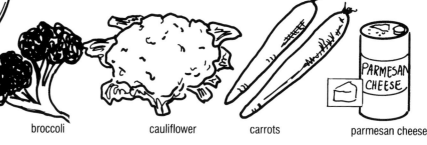

broccoli   cauliflower   carrots   parmesan cheese

lemon juice

nutmeg

1. Cut the tops off the broccoli. Measure 1 red cup.

2. Cut the cauliflower into pieces. Measure 1 red cup.

3. Rinse 1 red cup broccoli and 1 red cup cauliflower in cold water.

7. Put 1 red spoon water over the vegetables.

8. Cover the plate tightly with plastic wrap.

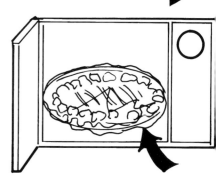

9. Put the vegetables in the microwave. Push **yellow**.

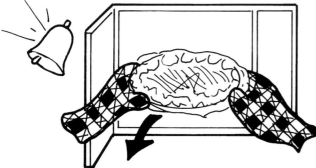

13. When the bell rings, put on oven mitts. Remove the vegetable plate from the microwave.

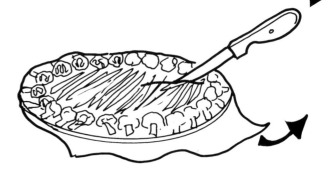

14. Use a knife to slit plastic wrap so steam escapes. Remove the plastic wrap.

6

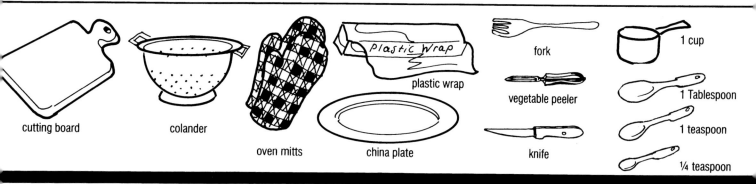

cutting board | colander | oven mitts | china plate | plastic wrap | fork | vegetable peeler | knife | 1 cup | 1 Tablespoon | 1 teaspoon | ¼ teaspoon

4. Peel the carrots.

5. Cut the carrots in half. Cut the halves into narrow strips.

6. Put the carrots in the middle of the plate. Put the cauliflower and broccoli around the outside with stems facing out.

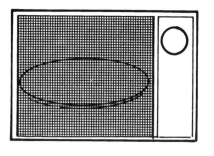
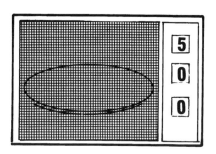
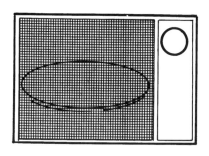

10. Push **blue**.

11. Push **5 0 0**.

12. Push **green**.

15. Sprinkle 1 yellow spoon lemon juice on the broccoli.

16. Sprinkle 1 yellow spoon parmesan cheese on the cauliflower.

17. Sprinkle 1 green spoon nutmeg on the carrots. Serve.

French Style Peas

salt pepper colander fork knife wooden spoon 1 cu

Tablespoo

1/2 teaspoo

1/4 teaspoo

frozen peas butter lettuce cutting board pot with lid

1. Rinse the lettuce.

2. Cut 1 red cup lettuce.

3. Put the pot on the stove. Turn to **yellow.**

4. Put 1 red spoon butter in the pot. Melt.

5. Add 1 red cup lettuce and 1 red cup frozen peas. Add 1 blue spoon salt and 1 green spoon pepper.

6. Stir.

5

OFF

7. Put the lid on the pot. Turn to **blue**.

8. Set the timer for 5 minutes.

9. When the bell rings, turn to **white**. Serve.

Cole Slaw

sugar • salt • pepper • lite mayonnaise • vinegar • onion • bowl • small bowl • wooden spoon • knife • fork • cutting board • grater • ½ cup • Tablespoon • 1 teaspoon • ¼ teaspoon • 8 oz. fresh cole slaw

1. Put the fresh cole slaw in the bowl.

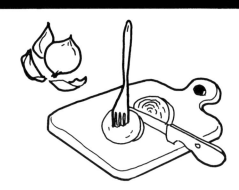

2. Peel the onion. Cut in half.

3. Put the fork into an onion half. Grate the onion.

4. Put 1 red spoon grated onion in the bowl.

5. Put 1 yellow cup lite mayonnaise in the bowl. Add 1 red spoon vinegar.

6. Add 1 yellow spoon sugar. Add 1 green spoon salt and 1 green spoon pepper.

7. Stir.

8. Pour dressing into the large bowl.

9. Stir. Serve.

orange | **1**

Spinach Salad

spinach • mushrooms • pepper • basil • colander • bowl • small bowl • Tablespoon • 1 teaspoon • lemon juice • mustard • olive oil • sugar • garlic powder • cutting board • knife • wooden spoon • fork • 1 cup • ½ teaspoon • ¼ teaspoon

1. Wash 3 red cups spinach.

2. Put the spinach in the bowl.

3. Wash 1 red cup mushrooms.

4. Slice the mushrooms

5. Add the mushrooms to the bowl.

6. Put 3 red spoons lemon juice and 2 yellow spoons olive oil in a small bowl.

7. Add 1 blue spoon basil and 1 green spoon garlic powder.

8. Add 1 blue spoon sugar and 1 green spoon pepper.

9. Add 1 green spoon mustard.

10. Beat with a fork.

11. Pour the dressing onto the salad. Stir. Serve.

2

Garden Salad

1 head lettuce

tomato

onion

celery

dressing

cutting board

bowl

colander

¼ cup

knife

1. Wash the lettuce, tomato and celery.

2. Tear lettuce to small pieces into the bowl.

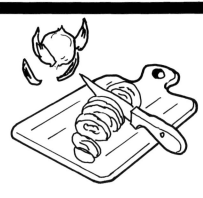

3. Peel and slice the onion.

4. Slice the celery.

5. Slice the tomato.

6. Add the tomato, celery and onion to the lettuce.

7. Shake the bottle of dressing.

8. Pour 1 green cup dressing over the salad. Serve.

Potato Salad

salt   pepper

parsley

4 potatoes

3 eggs

mayonnaise

mustard

vinegar

pot with lid

1. Wash the potatoes.

2. Pierce each potato.

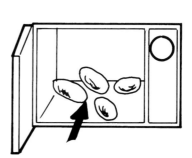

3. Put the potatoes in the microwave. Push **yellow**.

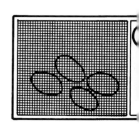

4. Push **blue**.

9. Put the pot on the stove. Turn to **red**.

10. When the water boils . . .

OFF

11. Put the lid on the pot. Turn to **white**.

15

12. Set the timer for 15 min

17. Cut the potatoes into cubes.

18. Put the potatoes into the bowl.

19. Put 1 yellow cup and 1 green cup mayonnaise into the small bowl. Add 2 red spoons mustard.

20. Add 1 red spoon parsley, 1 yellow spoon salt and 1 green spoon pepper.

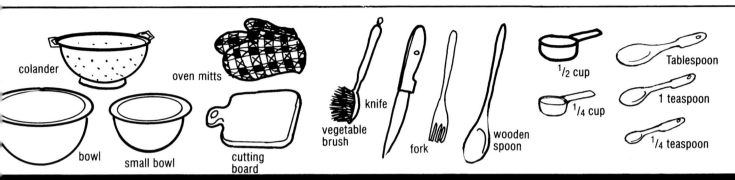

oven mitts

knife

vegetable brush

fork

wooden spoon

1/2 cup

1/4 cup

Tablespoon

1 teaspoon

1/4 teaspoon

bowl

small bowl

cutting board

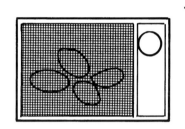

5. Push **2 0 0 0**.

6. Push **green**.

7. When the bell rings, put on oven mitts. Remove the potatoes.

8. Put 3 eggs in the pot. Cover with water.

13. When the bell rings, run cold water over the eggs.

14. Peel the eggs.

15. Chop the eggs.

16. Put the eggs in the bowl.

21. Add 1 red spoon vinegar.

22. Stir.

23. Pour the dressing over the potatoes.

24. Stir and serve.

5

Cranberry Sauce

Serves 8

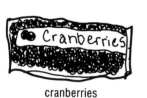
cranberries

sugar

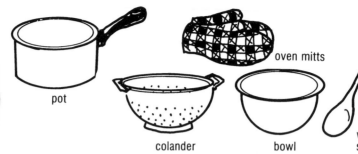
pot
colander
bowl
oven mitts
wooden spoon

1 cup
1/2 cup

1. Put 3 red cups cranberries in the colander. Wash.

2. Put the cranberries into the pot.

3. Add 1 red cup and 1 yellow cup water. Add 1 red cup sugar.

4. Put the pot on the stove. Turn to **red**.

10

5. Set the timer for 10 minutes.

6. Stir.

OFF

7. When the bell rings, turn to **white**.

8. Put on oven mitts. Pour the sauce into a bowl.

9. Refrigerate. Serve.

6 | orange

Impossible Pie

☺ ☺ ☺ ☺ ☺ ☺
Serves 6

Bisquick®   coconut   sugar   4 eggs   milk   rack   blender   1 cup   ½ cup   ¼ cup   1 teaspoon   vanilla   butter   10 inch pie pan   oven mitts

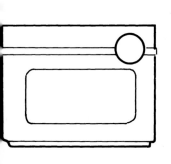

1. Preheat the oven. Turn to **blue**.

2. Put 2 red cups milk into the blender. Add 1 yellow cup and 1 green cup sugar.

3. Add 1 yellow cup Bisquick® and 4 eggs.

4. Add 1 green cup butter and 1 yellow spoon vanilla.

5. Put the lid on the blender. Blend.

6. Set the timer for 3 minutes.

7. When the bell rings, turn the blender off. Pour the mixture into the pie pan.

8. Sprinkle 1 red cup coconut on top.

9. Put on oven mitts. Put the pie into the oven.

10. Set the timer for 50 minutes.

11. When the bell rings, turn the oven to **white**. Put on oven mitts. Remove the pie.

12. Place on the rack to cool. Serve.

pink

Chocolate Chip Cookies

chocolate chips 6 oz.

sugar

butter

egg

vanilla

salt

brown sugar

baking soda

flour

oven mitts

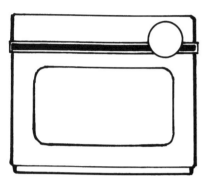

1. Preheat the oven. Turn to **yellow.**

2. Put 1 yellow cup butter, 1 blue cup sugar and 1 blue cup brown sugar into the mixing bowl.

3. Add 1 egg and 1 yellow spoon vanilla.

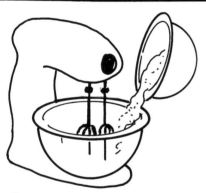

7. Add the dry ingredients to the mixer bowl.

8. Beat until well blended.

9. Add the chocolate chips.

12. Put on oven mitts. Place the cookie sheets in the oven.

13. Set the timer for 10 minutes.

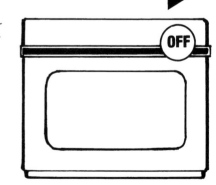

14. When the bell rings, turn the oven to **white.**

pink

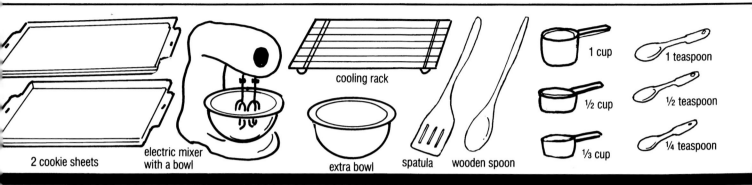

Serves a Crowd

2 cookie sheets | electric mixer with a bowl | cooling rack | extra bowl | spatula | wooden spoon | 1 cup | ½ cup | ⅓ cup | 1 teaspoon | ½ teaspoon | ¼ teaspoon

4. Beat until well blended.

5. Put 1 red cup flour, 1 blue spoon baking soda and 1 green spoon salt into another bowl.

6. Stir.

10. Stir.

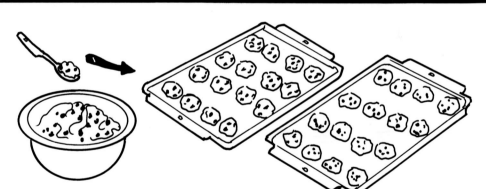

11. Put 1 rounded yellow spoon of dough in rows of 4 on both cookie sheets.

15. Put on oven mitts. Remove the cookie sheets.

16. Remove the cookies from the cookie sheets and place on the cooling rack. Serve.

pink

Apple Crumb Pie

6 apples

sugar

flour

brown sugar

butter

lemon juice

cinnamon

9" frozen pie shell

oven mitts

1. Put the baking sheet into the oven. Turn to **red**.

2. Peel the apples.

3. Core and slice the apples.

7. Add the apple slices.

8. Mix.

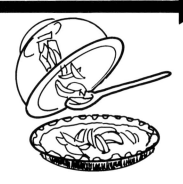

9. Spoon the apples into the pie shell.

Sprinkle the crumbs on the apples.

14. Put on oven mitts. Put the pie onto the baking sheet in the oven.

15. Set the timer for 40 minutes.

pink

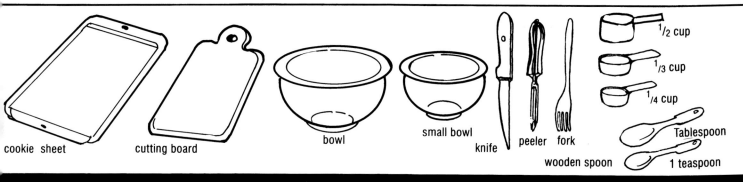

cookie sheet   cutting board   bowl   small bowl   knife   peeler   fork   wooden spoon

¹/₂ cup
¹/₃ cup
¹/₄ cup
Tablespoon
1 teaspoon

4. Put 2 blue cups sugar in the bowl. Add 2 red spoons flour.

5. Add 1 yellow spoon cinnamon and 1 red spoon lemon juice.

6. Stir.

10. Put 1 yellow cup flour in a small bowl. Add 1 green cup butter.

11. Add 1 green cup brown sugar.

12. Mix until crumbly.

16. When the bell rings, turn to **white**. Put on oven mitts. Remove the pie on the baking sheet.

55

17. Set the timer for 55 minutes.

18. When the bell rings, slice and serve.

Frozen Strawberry Drink

 Serves

vanilla

skim milk

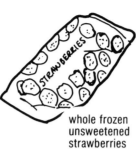
whole frozen
unsweetened
strawberries

sugar

glass

blender

1/2 cup

1/4 teaspoon

1 teaspoon

1. Put 1 yellow cup skim milk in the blender.

2. Add 1 yellow cup frozen strawberries.

3. Add 1 green spoon vanilla.

4. Add 1 yellow spoon sugar.

5. Put the lid on the blender.

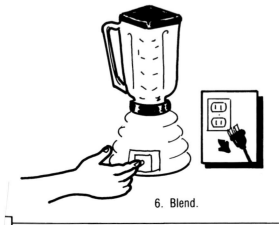
6. Blend.

7. When blended, pour into a glass. Serve.

5

pink

Mixed Fruit

banana　　apple　　orange　　grapes　　colander　　bowl　　cutting board　　knife　　fork　　wooden spoon

. Wash the apple and grapes.

2. Separate the grapes and put them into a bowl.

3. Peel and slice the banana.

4. Cut the apple in half. Core the apple.

5. Slice the apple.

6. Peel the orange. Separate into sections.

7. Cut the orange sections in half.

8. Put the pieces of banana, apple and orange into the bowl.

9. Stir and serve.

pink

Pumpkin Pie

30 oz. can pumpkin pie filling

2 eggs

evaporated milk

deep dish frozen pie shell

bowl

baking sheet

can opener

rack

wooden spoon

oven mitts

1/3 cup

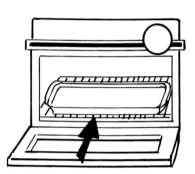

1. Put the baking sheet in the oven. Turn to **yellow**.

2. Break 2 eggs into a bowl. Beat.

3. Open the pumpkin pie filling and put it in the bowl.

4. Open the evaporated milk and pour 2 blue cups into the bowl.

5. Stir.

6. Pour the mix into a deep dish pie shell.

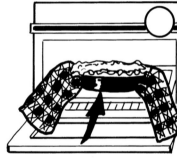

7. Put on oven mitts. Put the pie on the baking sheet in the oven.

55

8. Set the timer for _ minutes.

15

9. When the bell rings, set the timer for 15 minutes.

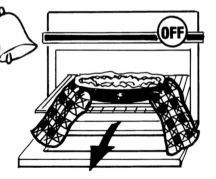

10. When the bell rings, put on oven mitts. Remove the pie.

11. Place the pie on a rack to cool. Serve.

pink

SUPPLEMENTAL RECIPES

- Scrambled Eggs
- Fried Eggs
- Bacon
- Oven French Toast
- Pancakes
- Egg Salad
- Quick Pizza Rolls
- Roast Cornish Hens

- Sirloin Steak
- Zucchini, Tomato & Onion
- Broccoli
- Mixed Vegetables
- Butternut Squash
- Cucumber Salad
- Fish Filets (two pages)

Published by Attainment Company, Inc., Verona, Wisconsin

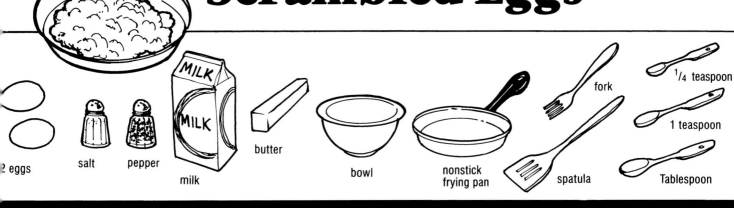

Scrambled Eggs

😊😊 **Serves 2**

2 eggs   salt   pepper   milk   butter   bowl   nonstick frying pan   spatula   fork   ¼ teaspoon   1 teaspoon   Tablespoon

1. Break 2 eggs into a bowl.

2. Add 2 red spoons milk and 1 green spoon salt.

3. Beat.

4. Put the pan on the stove. Turn to **yellow.**

5. Put 1 yellow spoon butter in the pan.

6. Pour the mixture into the pan.

7. Turn eggs until fluffy.

OFF

8. When eggs are cooked turn to **white.** Serve.

Fried Eggs

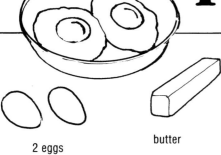

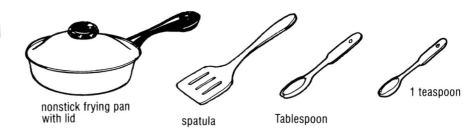

2 eggs   butter   nonstick frying pan with lid   spatula   Tablespoon   1 teaspoon

1. Put the pan on the stove. Turn to **yellow**.

2. Put 1 yellow spoon butter into the pan.

3. Crack the eggs into the pan.

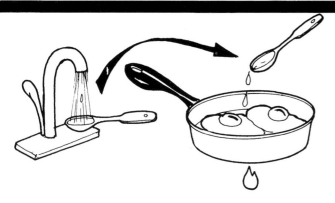

4. Add 1 red spoon water.

5. Put the lid on the pan. Turn to **blue**.

6. Set the timer for 3 minutes.

7. When the bell rings, turn to **white**.

8. Remove the eggs. Serve.

Bacon

bacon

china plate

paper towels

oven mitts

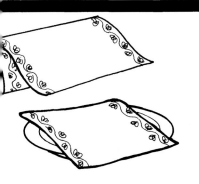

1. Put a paper towel on the plate.

2. Put 4 slices bacon on the paper towel.

3. Cover the bacon with another paper towel.

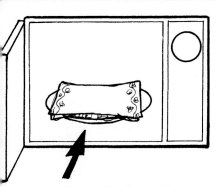

4. Put the plate in the microwave.

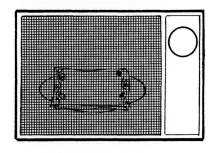

5. Close the door. Push **yellow**.

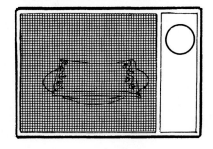

6. Push **blue**.

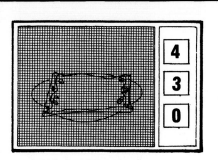

7. Push **4 3 0**.

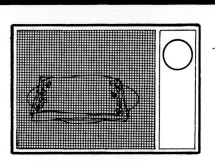

8. Push **green**.

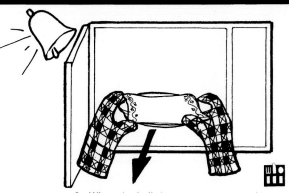

9. When the bell rings, put on oven mitts. Remove the bacon. Serve.

Oven French Toast

milk | 6 slices bread | 2 eggs | beater | oven mitts | bowl | nonstick baking sheet | spatula | ½ cup | fork

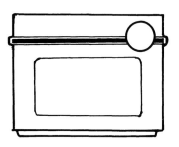

1. Preheat the oven. Turn to **red**.

2. Crack 2 eggs into the bowl. Add 1 yellow cup milk.

3. Beat.

4. Dip the bread into the mixture.

5. Place the bread on the baking sheet.

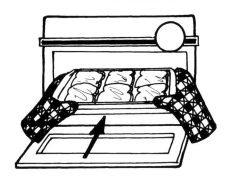

6. Put on oven mitts. Put the baking sheet into the oven.

7. Set the timer for 10 minutes.

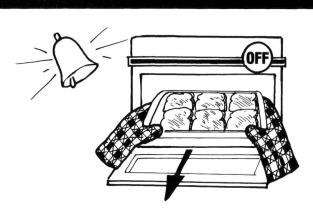

8. When the bell rings, turn to **white**. Put on the oven mitts. Remove the baking sheet.

9. Remove the French toast. Serve.

Serves 4

Pancakes

Bisquick®   2 eggs   oil   milk   bowl   beater   frying pan   spatula

1 cup
¼ cup
1 teaspoon

1. Put the frying pan on the stove. Turn to **yellow**.

2. Put 2 eggs in the bowl.

3. Add 2 red cups Bisquick®.

4. Add 1 red cup milk.

5. Beat.

6. Put 1 yellow spoon oil in the pan.

7. Pour 2 green cups batter.

8. When bubbles appear. . .

OFF

9. Turn to **white**. Remove pancakes. Repeat steps 5-9 for more pancakes.

Egg Salad

2 eggs   1 stalk celery   mayonnaise   pepper   pot   cutting board   bowl   fork   knife   Tablespoon   1/4 teaspoon

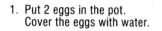

1. Put 2 eggs in the pot. Cover the eggs with water.

2. Put the pot on the stove. Turn to **red**.

3. When the water boils...

4. Cover the pot. Turn to **white**.

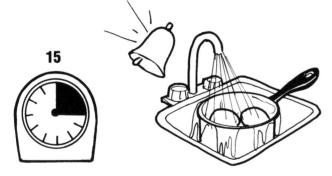

5. Set the timer for 15 minutes.

6. When the bell rings, run cold water over the eggs.

7. Peel the eggs.

8. Put the eggs in a bowl. Mash the egg

9. Rinse a stalk of celery.

10. Chop the celery.

11. Add the celery to the bowl. Add 1 red spoon mayonnaise and 1 green spoon pepper.

12. Stir and serve.

Quick Pizza Rolls

2 long Italian rolls

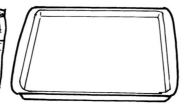

pizza sauce

shredded mozzarella

nonstick baking sheet

oven mitts

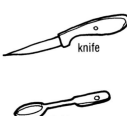

knife

Tablespoon

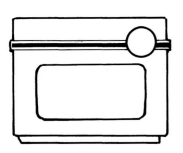

1. Preheat the oven. Turn to **red**.

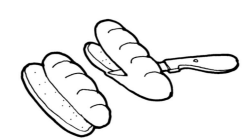

2. Cut the rolls lengthwise.

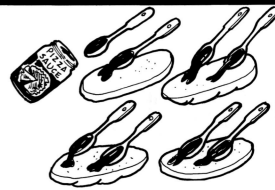

3. Spread 2 red spoons pizza sauce on each roll.

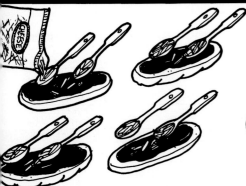

4. Spread 2 red spoons cheese on each roll.

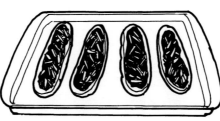

5. Put the rolls on a baking sheet.

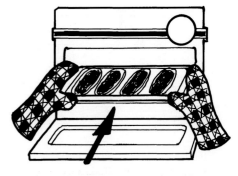

6. Put on oven mitts. Put the baking sheet in the oven.

10

7. Set the timer for 10 minutes.

8. When the bell rings, turn to **white**.

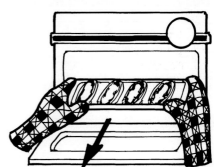

9. Put on the oven mitts. Remove the baking sheet. Serve.

Roast Cornish Hens

Serves

2 cornish hens   parsley   onion   2 ½ qt. glass baking dish   cutting board   fork   knife   oven mitts   colander

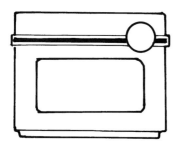

1. Preheat the oven. Turn to **red**.

2. Rinse the parsley.

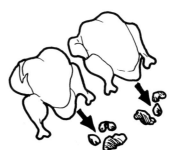

3. Remove the giblets.

4. Rinse the hens.

5. Peel the onion. Cut the onion in half.

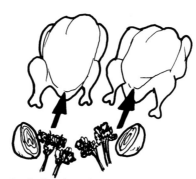

6. Put an onion half and parsley in each hen.

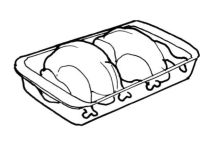

7. Put the hens into the baking dish.

8. Put on oven mitts. Put the dish in the oven.

55

9. Set the timer for 55 minutes.

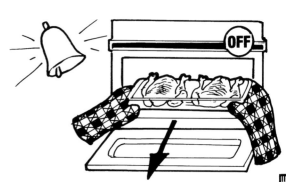

10. When the bell rings, turn to **white**. Put on oven mitts. Remove the hens. Serve.

Sirloin Steak

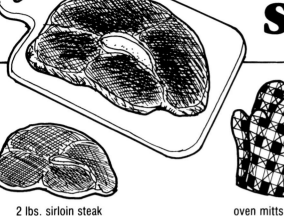

2 lbs. sirloin steak

oven mitts

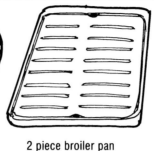

2 piece broiler pan

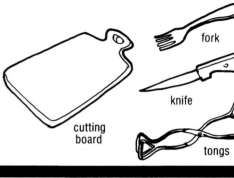

cutting board

fork

knife

tongs

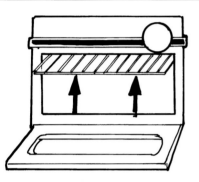
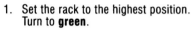

1. Set the rack to the highest position. Turn to **green**.

2. Put the steak on the broiler pan.

3. Put on oven mitts. Put the pan under the broiler.

10

4. Set the timer for 10 minutes.

5. When the bell rings, put on the oven mitts. Remove the pan.

6. Turn the steak over.

7. Return the pan to the broiler.

8

8. Set the timer for 8 minutes.

9. When the bell rings, turn to **white**. Put on oven mitts. Remove the pan.

10. Put steak on the cutting board. Cut into 4 sections. Serve.

Zucchini, Tomato and Onion

2 zucchini   pepper   onion   2 tomatoes   colander   cutting board   nonstick frying pan with lid   fork   knife   ¹/₄ teaspoon

1. Wash the zucchini and tomatoes.

2. Slice the tomatoes into chunks.

3. Slice the zucchini.

4. Peel and slice the onion.

5. Put the pan on the stove. Turn to **red**.

6. Put the tomatoes, zucchini and onion in the pan. Add 1 green spoon pepper.

7. Cover the pan. Turn to **blue**.

10

8. Set the timer for 10 minutes.

OFF

9. When the bell rings, turn to **white**. Serve.

Broccoli

1 bunch broccoli colander cutting board large pot with lid fork knife 1 cup

1. Rinse the broccoli.

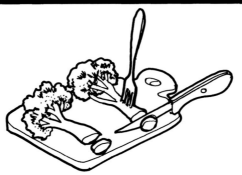

2. Cut the ends off the stems.

3. Cut the broccoli into pieces.

4. Put 4 red cups water into the pot.

5. Put the pot on the stove. Turn to **red**.

6. When the water boils...

7. Put the broccoli into the pot.

8. Put the lid on the pot. Turn to **blue**.

10

9. Set the timer for 10 minutes.

10. When the bell rings, turn to **white**.

Mixed Vegetables

oven mitts

16 oz. bag
mixed vegetables

glass
bowl

plastic wrap

Tablespoon

wooden spoon

knife

1. Put 2 red spoons water in a glass bowl.

2. Pour the frozen vegetables into the bowl.

3. Cover the bowl with plastic wrap.

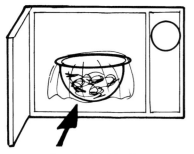

4. Put the bowl in the microwave. Close the door. Push **yellow**.

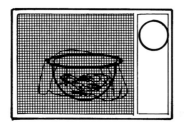

5. Push **blue**.

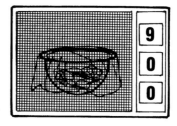

6. Push **9 0 0**.

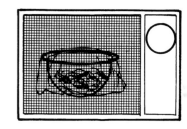

7. Push **green**.

8. When the bell rings, put on oven mitts. Remove the bowl.

9. Slit the plastic. Remove the plastic.

10. Stir. Serve.

Butternut Squash

😊 😊 😊 😊
Serves 4

butternut squash   cutting board   nonstick baking sheet   oven mitts   fork   spoon   knife

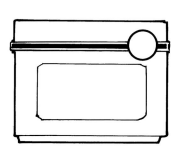
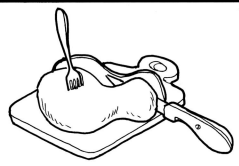
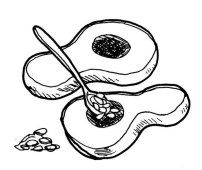

1. Preheat the oven. Turn to **red**.

2. Cut the squash in half.

3. Scoop out the seeds.

4. Place the squash cut side down on the baking sheet.

5. Put on the oven mitts. Put the baking sheet in the oven.

6. Set the timer for 45 minutes.

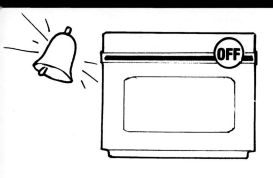

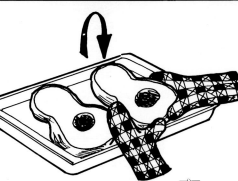

7. When the bell rings, turn to **white**.

8. Put on the oven mitts. Remove the squash.

9. Turn the squash. Serve.

Cucumber Salad

 Serves

cucumber plain yogurt vinegar pepper bowl fork knife wooden spoon ¹/₄ cup 1 teaspoon ¹/₄ teaspoon

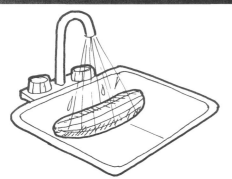

1. Rinse the cucumber.

2. Slice the cucumber.

3. Place the cucumber in the bowl.

4. Add 1 green cup yogurt.

5. Add 1 yellow spoon vinegar.

6. Add 1 green spoon pepper.

7. Stir and serve.

Fish Filets

4 fish filets (1lb.)

lemon juice

salt

pepper

parsley

butter

2 qt. glass baking dish

1. Put a fish filet in each corner of a glass dish. Turn under the thin ends.

2. Put 1 green cup butter in the glass measuring cup.

3. Put the cup in the microwave.

8. When the bell rings, put on the oven mitts. Remove the cup.

9. Put 1 red spoon lemon juice in the cup. Add 1 blue spoon salt and 1 green spoon pepper.

10. Chop the parsley. Measure 1 green cup.

14. Put the dish into the microwave.

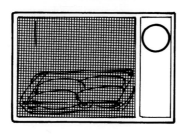

15. Close the door. Push **yellow**.

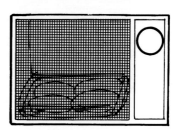

16. Push **blue**.

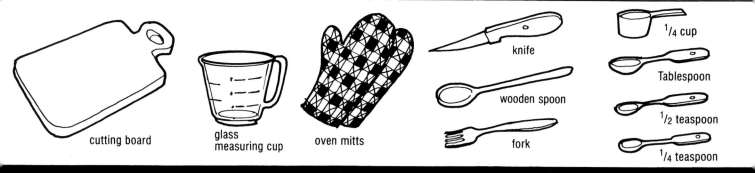

cutting board
glass measuring cup
oven mitts
knife
wooden spoon
fork
$^1/_4$ cup
Tablespoon
$^1/_2$ teaspoon
$^1/_4$ teaspoon

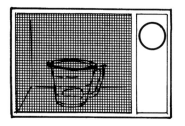

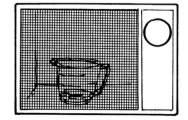

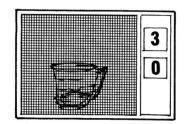

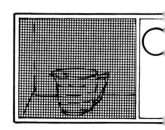

4. Close the door. Push **yellow**.

5. Push **blue**.

6. Push **3 0**.

7. Push **green**.

11. Add 1 green cup parsley to the cup.

12. Stir.

13. Pour the mixture over the fish.

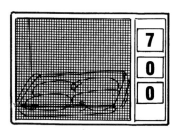

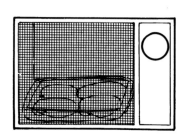

17. Push **7 0 0**.

18. Push **green**.

19. When the bell rings, put on oven mitts. Remove the dish. Serve.